The British Heart Foundation was created as the first body of its kind in the United Kingdom which aims to finance cardiovascular research. Formed under the patronage of H.R.H. Prince Philip, it enjoys the full support of the leading United Kingdom medical authorities.

Entirely dependent on voluntary contributions the British Heart Foundation has in recent years awarded grants totalling several million pounds to a large number of vital research programmes. In addition, it has to date endowed nine professorial Chairs in cardiovascular diseases at universities throughout the country. Post-graduate educational work is undertaken in order to ensure that doctors and nurses are kept fully informed on developments leading to improved treatment. Grants are provided in special circumstances to enable hospitals to improve facilities for treating patients.

Britain has played an outstanding role in world heart research and much of this has only been possible through the efforts of the British Heart Foundation. The Foundation ensures that this tradition continues, both by financing promising research in this country and by maintaining close links with similar bodies overseas. This is a fine record, but as the cost and amount of research grows, so does the level of support required from the Foundation.

The British Heart Foundation publishes a useful series of leaflets designed to give advice and encouragement to those who suffer from diseases of the heart and circulation. These are available free of charge and principal leaflets are listed below:

Where Do You Go From Here?
Advice for those who have suffered a
Coronary Thrombosis
Success in Heart Research
Recovery From a Stroke
What is Angina?
Congenital Heart Disease
Modern Heart Medicines
How to Control Your Weight and
The Facts about Cholesterol

High Blood Pressure

All these items are available from:–

British Heart Foundation,
57 Gloucester Place,
London W1H 4DH

THE OFFICIAL BRITISH HEART FOUNDATION COOKBOOK

Cooking

EDITED BY KATIE DYSON

for your Heart's Content

D. Wainwright Evans, M.D., B.Sc., F.R.C.P.
and Meta A. M. Greenfield, S.R.D.
Consultant Cardiologist and Senior Dietitian
at Addenbrooke's Hospital, Cambridge

Hutchinson of London

Acknowledgements

Thanks are due to the following for their help in preparing this book:

ICI PHARMACEUTICALS
THE FLOUR ADVISORY BUREAU – for recipes and preparing food for photography
MAZOLA CORN OIL LTD – for recipes
KNORR LTD – for recipes
BROWN AND POLSON LTD – for recipes
DR D. A. T. SOUTHGATE, THE DUNN NUTRITIONAL LABORATORY, CAMBRIDGE
THE DIETITIANS GROUP AT ADDENBROOKE'S HOSPITAL
VAN DEN BERGHS LTD – for recipes
EDEN VALE LTD – for recipes
DAVIS GELATINE LTD – for recipes
LUCY HEDLEY – for recipes
J. BIBBY & SONS LTD – for recipes
ALISON BOYD – for recipes
AMERICAN HEART ASSOCIATION – for recipes

Credits

Colour photography by Clive Corless
Line drawings by Kate Simunek
Cooking pots, glass and oven dishes from a selection at
    Yvonne Peters, Barnes High Street, SW13, and Selfridges
Fresh vegetables and salad foods from Robert Jackson, Piccadilly

Hutchinson & Co (Publishers) Ltd
3 Fitzroy Square, London W1
London Melbourne Sydney Auckland
Wellington Johannesburg and agencies
throughout the world

First published 1976
Second impression 1977
© British Heart Foundation 1977

Designed and produced by
Hutchinson Benham Ltd
Printed in Great Britain by litho by
The Anchor Press Ltd
and bound by Wm Brendon & Son Ltd
both of Tiptree, Essex

ISBN 0 09 127530 X

Contents

Foreword

The following recipes offer a wide range of dishes – many of them in daily use – suitable for those who wish to minimize their risk of developing heart and circulatory disease. With these recipes it is simple to control fat and cholesterol intake without having to weigh every piece of food. They have been designed to make the food exciting and delicious and therefore should be attractive to all who wish to derive maximum enjoyment from their food, with a minimum risk for the future. The dishes will also appeal to those who have suffered a coronary attack, or who have arterial disease elsewhere, and have been advised to follow a diet designed to lower blood cholesterol levels.

Where excess weight is part of the problem, the total amount of food eaten must be carefully watched. Recipes most useful to slimmers are clearly marked in the book and the chart on page 124 provides a quick guide to the more suitable foods. If you already follow a medically-designed diet, keep to your own personal instructions.

The main aim of the British Heart Foundation is to finance and support research into the causes, prevention and treatment of diseases of the heart and circulation; ample reason for it to sponsor and highly recommend this book.

British Heart Foundation,
57 Gloucester Place, London W1H 4DH

Medical Introduction

Coronary heart disease, or ischaemic heart disease (IHD), is by far the biggest killer in our modern society. In England and Wales it caused the deaths of over 150 000 men and women[1] in 1973. Among men over the age of thirty-five, deaths from this cause exceeded deaths from all forms of cancer combined. Behind this stark mortality lurks the spectre of a restricted life for some of those whose hearts keep going after narrowing of the coronary arteries (the heart's own source of nutrition) has developed to a critical stage. All too often, this can mean unacceptable limitation of a man's life-style just at the time of his peak success and productivity.

While we are still far from a complete understanding of all the mechanisms involved in coronary heart disease and its various manifestations, there is already sufficient knowledge of major factors involved to give real hope that prevention of most premature coronary attacks may be feasible. Indeed, the recent downturn in the coronary death rate in the USA may reflect the success of public education efforts there, particularly with regard to smoking.[2]

Those seriously intent on minimizing their chances of falling victim to coronary heart disease, as well as to other diseases, will surely be non-smokers. They will also take advantage of any facilities for blood pressure checks at work or elsewhere. The third major factor is diet; appropriate action in this respect involves avoidance of obesity and reduction in the amount of fat consumed,[3] especially 'saturated fat'. This is fat in which the fatty acids have no double-bond linkages in their carbon chains. Fortunately it isn't necessary to understand Chemistry in order to avoid such fats; it is almost enough to know that dairy fats and most others of animal origin are rich in them. This book is about the ways and means of eating less of these fats.

1. Registrar General's Statistical Review of England and Wales for the year 1973, HMSO, 1975.

2. Stamler, J., *Bulletin of the International Society of Cardiology*, ISC, Geneva, Summer 1975, page 5.
3. *Diet and Coronary Heart Disease*, HMSO, 1974, page 23.

In general terms, it is healthy to take regular, sensible exercise and the avoidance of stress is frequently advised. However, it is difficult to alter one's basic personality, standards or *raison d'être*, and for most responsible middle-aged men all that can reasonably be hoped for is the development of a certain 'philosophy of maturity'. This can usefully include a realistic appraisal of remaining ambitions and the abandonment of juvenile racetrack attitudes when driving.

Other factors apart, an habitually high consumption of saturated fat is considered by some to be a *necessary* factor in the development of coronary heart disease.[4] It may explain the very high incidence of coronary disease amongst the bucolic Finns as contrasted with the low incidence among the highly stressed Japanese. The mechanism by which it favours arterial deposits and narrowing need not concern us here. Suffice it to say that the blood concentration of a substance called cholesterol appears to be an essential link or index and that fat of this type tends to increase it. To a lesser extent the amount of cholesterol itself in the diet is also involved. Vegetable and marine fats composed chiefly of unsaturated fats have either no effect on blood cholesterol or tend to reduce it.

A prudent diet, therefore, avoids excessive intake of food generally and involves reduction of saturated fat and cholesterol intake to an acceptable minimum. No more than a third of one's daily energy intake should be in the form of fat and at least half of this fat should be in the unsaturated form. In practice this means cutting out certain foods (especially dairy foods) altogether, while curtailing others and substituting alternatives. For example, one should forsake cream for ever, or at least feel deliciously guilty when, very exceptionally, falling to its temptation. Most cheeses and the obvious fat on meat should likewise be avoided. Butter and cooking fats of animal origin should be replaced by a suitable margarine or oil and full-cream milk by the skimmed variety. Full details of the eating pattern are given in the next section, written by a dietitian long experienced in the practicalities of managing such wholesale changes within the family setting.

The recipes in this book were designed and collected to show that an interesting and varied diet can be enjoyed by those intent on keeping their blood cholesterol levels down. There is, incidentally, no virtue in deliberately consuming large quantities of unsaturated fat. This would surely lead to weight gain and be counter-productive (as is over-consumption of sugar, alcohol or any other food).

The degree of enthusiasm for these changes will vary with individual circumstances. People with identified high blood cholesterol problems are usually well motivated and should be under medical and dietetic care. It is hoped that these recipes will, if considered suitable by their advisers, help them to adhere to what might otherwise seem a monotonous diet. Fortunately, after a few months, there is often a striking change in food preferences so that fatty dishes are instinctively avoided. This greatly simplifies the problems of eating out, though these problems can be exaggerated. An occasional, truly exceptional, excess intake of saturated fat is of no material consequence. It is a low average consumption of fat over years or decades that really matters, for the influence of diet in the causation of coronary heart disease is probably very long-term. For this reason it is hoped that at least some of the general population, and not just those known to be at special risk, may be influenced by the contents of this book to adopt and maintain a more prudent diet throughout adult life.

David Wainwright Evans
Consultant Cardiologist, Addenbrooke's Hospital
Cambridge

Note to the Second Edition

Since the above was written, the Joint Working Party of the Royal College of Physicians and the British Cardiac Society has published its report. Its dietary recommendations for the whole community[5] are essentially similar and should add impetus to the really long-term prevention exercise.

David Wainwright Evans
Cambridge   *February 1977*

4. Blackburn, H., *Progress in Cardiology (3)* (Ed. Yu and Goodwin), Lea and Febiger, Philadelphia, 1974, page 7.
5. *Prevention of Coronary Heart Disease*, J.Roy, Coll.Phycns., 1976, Vol. 10, page 2.

The Good Hearted Diet

USEFUL TERMS

When starting a good hearted diet, it helps to understand some of the terms you may meet. It is important to learn about fats so that you know which types are found in the different foods you eat.

Carbohydrates These are found in starchy and sugary foods. They supply short-term energy for the body because they are digested quickly, especially sugar and glucose. Specifically they are:

Sugar: Sugar itself, glucose, syrup, treacle, jam and marmalade, sweet soft drinks.

Starches: Bread, cereals, flour, and products made with flour, potatoes, rice, maize, pasta.

Milk sugar: All milks, including skimmed milk, contain the carbohydrate called lactose.

Fruit sugar: The carbohydrate fructose is found in all fruits and honey.

Cholesterol This substance is normally present in the blood and is manufactured by the body. It is also obtained from foods. The levels of blood cholesterol vary widely in different parts of the world, depending mainly on local eating habits. A raised cholesterol level is implicated in coronary heart disease, plaques containing cholesterol being found in the walls of the arteries. Foods containing cholesterol come in five groups:

Cholesterol-free: All plants and vegetables and their products.

Low cholesterol: Skimmed milk and low fat yoghurt.

Medium cholesterol: White fish – cod, haddock, sole, plaice, whiting, etc. (including smoked haddock).
Oily fish – herrings, kippers, mackerel, tuna, salmon, sardines, lobster.
Meat – lean cuts of beef, lamb, pork, chicken, turkey, rabbit, ham, oxtail, corned beef, lean tinned meats.
Dairy products – milk, cheese, except Stilton and Cheddar.

Medium-high cholesterol: These contain two to four times as much cholesterol as food in the medium group: heart, ox or pig's liver, lamb's tongue, tripe, shrimps, prawns, cream, Stilton and Cheddar cheeses, whole egg.

High cholesterol: These contain over four times as much cholesterol as the medium group: egg yolk, brain, calf, chicken and lamb's liver, sweetbreads, fish roes.

Energy The energy that food supplies is measured in units called *Calories.* Their full name is kilocalories. (When kilojoules replace them, the conversion factor will be 4·2 KJ = 1 Cal.) Protein, fat and carbohydrates all supply calories, but fat is the most concentrated source. It supplies two and a quarter times as much energy as the other two.

Fats These give long-term energy because they take longer to be digested and absorbed into the system. They are found in foods as:

Visible obvious fats like lard, suet, cooking fat, oil, butter, margarine, fat on meat and cream.

Invisible fats like milk, fat in meat, cheese, oily fish. Small quantities are contained in cereals. Vegetables and fruit, apart from avocado pears and olives, contain a minimal amount of fat.

When chemically analysed, fats contain, as part of their make-up, substances known as fatty acids. These come in three types:

Saturated fatty acids: these are found in foods of mainly animal origin. Over long periods eating too much food containing saturated fatty acids tends to increase blood cholesterol levels. These fats are found in: cream, cheese, milk fat, butter, meat fat, cooking fat, dripping, lard, suet, coconut and palm oils, cocoa and chocolate; hard and soft margarines which are not specifically polyunsaturated.

Mono-unsaturated fatty acids: these neither raise nor lower the blood cholesterol levels. However, they do add to the total daily fat (and energy) intake. Foods containing them also have some saturated fatty acids as well. They are found in largest amounts in: olive oil, peanut oil, olives, avocado pears.

Polyunsaturated fatty acids: these tend to lower the blood cholesterol level. They are usually liquid oils extracted from plant seeds such as safflower, sunflower, corn and soya bean. Polyunsaturated margarines are a convenient source of this type of fatty acid. It is important to remember that even the most highly polyunsaturated oil – safflower – is only 72 per cent 'poly', the rest being 'mono' and saturated fat. The best soft margarines are about 50 per cent 'poly', the rest being 'mono' and saturated.

Proteins   These are the main body building and repair foods. The best quality and most concentrated sources are found in meat, fish, cheese, milk, eggs, nuts and soya beans. The now fashionable textured vegetable proteins are extracted from soya beans and field beans. Then come the medium sources in quality and concentration: wheat flour, bread, wheat cereals, peas, broad beans, lentils, haricot and other dried beans. All protein supplying foods are a mixture of protein and fat and/or carbohydrate.

Triglycerides   These are also normally found in the blood. The body uses them for carrying fatty acids. Raised levels are usually associated with obesity and/or abnormal handling of carbohydrate by the body.

CHOOSING YOUR FOOD: HOW TO USE THE DIET

This section makes it simple for you to select the right foods for good-hearted eating.

Meat

Meat contains a great deal of invisible as well as visible fat, so meat portions must be small. Buy only lean cuts and beware of meat with too much fat marbled through it. Trim off all excess fat. If you always choose very carefully and trim before cooking, economical cuts can be used just as well as the more expensive ones. When buying minced beef, choose lean shin or chuck steak and ask your butcher to mince it. If this is not possible, buy the best quality mince and strain off all the fat produced after browning the meat. Avoid fatty tinned or prepared meats like luncheon meat, salami and sausages. Make certain that lamb, pork, ham or bacon really are lean. Pork, although it contains a little more fat than beef or lamb, contains a higher proportion of polyunsaturated fat. Offal – kidneys, liver, etc. – is normally banned because it is high in cholesterol.

Poultry or White Meat

Chicken, turkey and rabbit contain less fat than other meats so can be eaten in larger portions. Beware of duck and goose, which are high in fat.

Fish

White fish, lobster and smoked haddock have a minimal fat content and can be eaten freely. Oily fish like herrings, mackerel, pilchards, tuna and salmon, have as much fat as lean meat, but are low in saturated fat. Apart from lobster and scampi, all shellfish and fish roes are high in cholesterol, so should be avoided.

Dairy Produce

Avoid full cream milk, especially Jersey (gold top) and homogenised (red top). Use skimmed milk, either as a powder made up into a liquid, or fresh skimmed milk, if it is available. A few dairies will supply this to order. If skimmed milk is not available at work or on holiday, a small amount of fresh milk with the cream siphoned off may be used. Omit cream, butter, Cheddar, Stilton, Danish Blue and cream cheese of all types because the fat content is very high. However, Dutch Edam and Gouda may occasionally be substituted for a small quantity of meat. Use cottage cheese freely as this is low in fat – the same applies to low fat yoghurt. Most plain well-known makes of ice cream contain only a little fat in small portions, so can be used 2–3 times a week, but avoid the richer types, including Cornish. Also avoid coffee creamers.

Eggs

Egg yolks are very high in cholesterol. On a low cholesterol diet, reduce these to one a week. Substitute liver for this one egg occasionally, because it is an invaluable source of concentrated iron and vitamins – especially important for children and women of child-bearing years. Liver is normally forbidden because of its high cholesterol content. Have *as many egg whites as you want*. They are allowed freely.

Fats and Oils

For cooking, use oils. The ones containing the greatest number of polyunsaturated fats are listed first: safflower, sunflower, soya bean, corn. Don't buy oils labelled anonymously 'vegetable oil'. Instead, choose one with the seed oil content on the label. Although oil is used a great deal in these recipes, remember that your total fat intake should be rationed, especially if you are slimming. Avoid peanut (groundnut), olive and coconut oils.

Margarine: use a brand which states it is 'high in polyunsaturates'. These are usually about 50 per cent polyunsaturated. Other soft margarines fall into two groups, either about 30 per cent or about 15 per cent polyunsaturated, but it is not possible to state a named list as they can vary from season to season.

Sauces and Salad Dressings

Some of the ready-made brands may be suitable. Be sure to read the labelled contents carefully first because the oil used may vary depending on the variety available to the manufacturer.

Vegetables and Fruits

Use all vegetables and fruits freely, except for avocado pears and olives. Pulse vegetables are good suppliers of protein and iron, economical, filling and low in fat. This group includes fresh, frozen, tinned or dried peas, broad beans, lentils, haricot beans, baked beans, black eye and kidney beans. Dried peas, lentils and beans make good soups and help to fill out meat portions in stews and casseroles. A wide variety of these can be obtained from specialist grocers or health food shops. Textured vegetable protein, made from soya and field beans, can also be used as there is a low saturated fat content. Slimmers should steer clear of vegetables that are high in calories like potatoes, sweetcorn, tinned and processed peas, haricot beans and lentils.

Proprietary Foods

Most of these are unsuitable. Read package labels carefully to check if they contain unsaturated fats. Remember that labels have to list ingredients in order of quantity. The ingredient present in largest quantity is always listed first. Some plain biscuits like water biscuits or matzos and some crispbreads can be included. If you are on a prescribed diet, check first with your dietitian. Bought cakes, pastries and 'take away' foods including fish and chips, unless known to be cooked with the correct margarine or oil, are not suitable.

Sugar, Desserts and Alcohol

Sugar, jam, marmalade, syrup and sugary soft drinks, as well as alcohol, should all be used in moderation. This group should be more severely restricted if blood triglycerides are high or if you are overweight.

Advice for Slimmers

Many of the extra calories in the recipes found in this book come from carbohydrate foods like potatoes, pasta, rice and flour, or from the special cooking oil or margarine. It is easy to reduce the calorie value. Either use oil or margarine merely to grease the pan before browning meat, or use a non-stick pan. This will save 264 calories per 30 ml (1 fl. oz) of oil, and 226 calories per 30 g (1 oz) of margarine. Omit the oil from French dressing and make a slimmer's version from vinegar and seasonings, or the juice of a fresh lemon, adding a crushed clove of garlic or a pinch of mustard for extra bite. Remember, you are allowed a certain amount of oil or margarine each day, which can be accounted for in the recipes.

Thickenings, like cornflour or flour, can easily be left out of stews, and other dishes like vegetable soups, making a calorie saving of 100 per 30 g (1 oz). If rice, pasta and potato are included in the recipe, serve only your allowed portion from the day's carbohydrate ration. Subtract the calories removed (i.e. the thickening or oil, margarine) from the total number of calories given for the recipe. Divide the remainder by the number of servings. If the calories for a main course are about 200–250 per serving, this is suitable for slimmers. A helpful list of food portions for slimmers can be found in the appendix on page 125. Also the chart on page 124 gives a speedy guide to choosing the right foods to help you lose weight.

Advice for Diabetics and Those Restricting Carbohydrates

Some people may be on a 'carbohydrate exchange' type of restricted diet. This will include many diabetics. These are different from calorie restricted diets as only the carbohydrates are being counted while varying protein and fat content of foods will alter the calories considerably. Eating portions are worked out in terms of 10 g carbohydrates (C). These portions can be interchanged to vary daily eating. Adapt the recipes by omitting or counting the thickening in main course dishes, soups and so on, so they have the appropriate amount of carbohydrates from potatoes, rice and pasta to conform with your individual allowance. Although you will have your own portion list, there is also one on page 125 which will help you to use these recipes. Before adapting these recipes, it is wise to consult your dietitian.

Advice for People With Stomach Disorders

People suffering from stomach or duodenal ulcers, or from hiatus hernia, can easily adapt this diet to their needs. General advice is to eat small meals regularly; do not go a long time without food; avoid all fried food; use oil or special margarine in cookery for stews, soups, and French dressings. Increase your skimmed milk, low fat yoghurt and cottage cheese allowance if you need more milky foods. Bran, often advised for diverticular disease or constipation, can be used with this diet. Anyone wishing to increase 'roughage' in daily eating, can add a tablespoon of bran to their breakfast cereal each morning.

Vegetarian Diets

It is relatively easy for vegetarians to follow a good hearted diet, especially if the basis of their diet is pulse vegetables like peas, dried beans, lentils, etc., or textured vegetable protein. But it is more of a problem if egg and cheese are the mainstay of the diet. However, many cheeses are not higher in cholesterol and saturated fat than meat, so can be eaten instead of it. Try to keep the egg intake down to 3–4 a week, and try to introduce more of the pulse vegetables as a suitable alternative protein source.

EATING OUT

This can present problems for any dieter. However, an occasional blow-out does little harm, especially if you make up afterwards by taking special care. A suitable meal can usually be chosen from a restaurant menu. Fruit juices, melon, grapefruit, other fruit cocktails and consommé soups are all free of fat and cholesterol. Choose plain meat and fish dishes, avoiding rich concoctions. Don't choose dishes with rich sauces. Vegetables, salads without dressing, potatoes, rice, etc., are fine, but avoid fried, roast or chipped potatoes where possible. Don't choose rich creamy sweet dishes. Instead go for fruit, ice creams or sorbets, which are a safer bet.

If you are on an especially rigid diet and are eating at a friend's home, it is worth contacting your hostess first for a tactful discussion. This saves her embarrassment if you are unable to eat her meal. When visiting friends or staying in an hotel, remember to say what you can eat. Don't just reel off a long list of banned food – it is very off-putting to a hostess or hotel staff.

PREPARING AND COOKING YOUR FOOD

It is important to remove all visible fats before cooking – this applies to poultry as well as red meat. Minimize the fat content in stocks, soups and stews or casseroles by skimming the fat off occasionally during cooking. Allow the dish to cool after cooking, then remove any fat after it has solidified – it is easier this way and you can get rid of the fat more efficiently. *Always* substitute oil and polyunsaturated margarine for other fats when cooking. Many of your own recipes can easily be adapted. Simply use polyunsaturated oils and fats instead of butter or lard as in the original recipe.

Use cooking methods which remove fat, like baking, boiling, grilling, roasting and stewing. When roasting meats, place the joint on a rack, then put this in the roasting tin. Add a little oil, marinade, stock, or tomato juice to keep it moist – not meat fat or dripping. Then cover with foil. The foil helps to keep the meat moist without basting, and reduces shrinkage in roast meat, especially if a small joint is being cooked. An alternative way is to place the meat on a rack in a covered roasting pan – this works out more economically in the long run than buying foil. Always pour off all the fat from the tin after cooking and make the gravy from the brownings of the meat. A double-lipped gravy boat with a deep funnel at one end to pour the stock from under any surface fat is a great help. Cook roast vegetables and Yorkshire pudding in oil in separate tins.

Do not overheat cooking oil. It reaches much higher temperatures before smoking than other fats so food added at this temperature burns on the outside before it is cooked on the inside. Do not add food to oil which is not hot enough, otherwise it absorbs too much fat and tastes greasy and indigestible. Test the temperature by frying a cube of bread first. This should turn nicely brown and crisp in 30 seconds. Whenever possible use shallow frying methods with oil. Always use fresh oil each time. An efficient non-stick frying pan helps, because it needs little or no oil. After cooking, excess fat should be removed by draining the food on kitchen paper. Use oil when making French dressing, mayonnaise, marinades, sauces, and cakes and scones, as well as pastry. It does not take long to use up your daily oil allowance – be careful it is not exceeded.

Aim to adapt the family meals to the needs of the diet, so that double cooking is only necessary occasionally, otherwise the diet becomes a chore, not merely the modification of a way of life. Remember that growing children need more vitamins and minerals in proportion to their size than adults do. Some foods not allowed on this diet should be included for children, like unskimmed milk, egg yolks and liver, which are good sources of iron and vitamins A, B and D.

Using up excess egg yolks need not be a problem. Some can be used to make egg custards or egg yolk mayonnaise for special occasions. If you really are stuck with the extra yolks, they can be used outside the kitchen. Egg yolk is a popular beauty aid. It makes a good hair conditioner. Mix with a little lemon juice, rub into the hair after washing and rinse with *luke-warm* water.

Cottage cheese can be used successfully for cooking as a topping for pizzas, in soups and for snack dishes. It is easy to pep up the taste if you are using it on its own by adding chopped fresh herbs, seasonings and mustards.

Use your ingredients like a painter's palette. Experiment to invent your own recipes or embellish existing ones in your own way. Good cooking does not necessarily mean that everything should be smothered in cream, egg yolks and butter. The new cooking style in France, pioneered by Chef Michel Guerard, shuns these old *Cordon bleu* favourites. Instead he uses gently cooked vegetables puréed to a cream, concentrating on cutting down the unnecessary calories. His foods are often cooked quickly and simply to bring out maximum flavour without suffocating in fat. Experimental cooking of this type is fun to do if there is a bit of spare time, and well worth while if you can add your own individual touches to everyday eating.

Meta A. M. Greenfield, s.r.d.
Senior Dietitian, Addenbrooke's Hospital
Cambridge

Breakfasts

Breakfast should be a light meal for the good hearted diet. Concentrate on fresh fruit and cereals, not the traditional cooked breakfast. If you crave for bacon and eggs, it can be worth using the weekly allowance of one whole egg for a special Sunday-morning treat. Cook the egg in your favourite way, perhaps boiled, or fried in oil with grilled bacon and tomatoes. In cold weather, eat cooked fish for a warm start to the day. Have your usual morning tea or coffee, but with skimmed milk and preferably without sugar. Add a daily tablespoonful of bran to breakfast cereal to pep up the digestive system and keep it running smoothly. Apart from home-made fruit juices, bought varieties are also good for breakfasts, but always check the ingredients on the label first.

Breakfast kedgeree

115 g (4 oz) rice
170 g (6 oz) cooked smoked haddock
1 tablespoon cooking oil
seasoning
1 hard-boiled egg white, chopped
fresh chopped parsley

771 calories
Cook rice, flake fish. Place oil in pan, add seasoning, egg white, rice and flaked fish. Heat thoroughly. Mix in the parsley, reserving some for garnish. *Serves 2.*

Muesli

8 parts flaked or rolled oats
1 part wheat germ
1 part chopped dates
1 part dried apple
1 part dried apricot
1 part sultanas
1 part skimmed milk powder
1 part soft brown sugar (optional)
1–2 parts bran

Use a biscuit tin with a tight lid to store the muesli, which can be made in bulk. The oats are the basis. Choose any or all of the other ingredients to suit your taste, and combine everything together in the biscuit tin. Eat either with skimmed milk or, often more refreshingly, with unsweetened orange juice from a tin or carton.

Breakfast baked fish

450 g (1 lb) white fish fillets or smoked
    haddock
140 ml (¼ pt) skimmed milk
½ teaspoon polyunsaturated margarine
seasoning
small bay leaf (optional)

Suitable for slimmers   525 calories
Place fish and skimmed milk in baking dish. Dot
with margarine. Season well, add bay leaf, and bake
in a covered dish for 20 minutes, using a moderate
oven, 375°F, 190°C, Mark 5.   *Serves 4.*

Breakfast lemon drink

1 lemon
1 teaspoon clear honey
    or use artificial sweetener
1 cup hot water

With honey: 47 calories Suitable for slimmers
with sweetener: minimum calories
Squeeze lemon into glass. Add honey, then stir
with teaspoon and pour hot water on top. This
healthy drink makes a refreshing start first thing in
the morning. As an added bonus, the lemon is said
to help keep the complexion clear.

Home-made tomato juice

900 g (2 lb) firm ripe tomatoes
2 tablespoons water
salt

Suitable for slimmers   126 calories
Wash tomatoes, cut out stems, remove any soft
spots and chop roughly. Add water to pan and
simmer gently until soft, about 5–10 minutes. Put
through fine sieve. Return to pan, add salt and heat
to boiling point. Place in covered jar or bottle and
keep in refrigerator. Serve with Worcestershire
sauce. With an electric juicer, the fresh juice can be
extracted from the tomatoes without cooking.
Serves 6.

Soups and Starters

Fresh home-made soup is one of the best beginnings to any meal. Soup does not need to be laced with cream to be good. Fresh vegetables gently cooked with a subtle home-made stock, then puréed until they are smooth and creamy textured, taste delicious. Stock cubes are great helpers if you are short of time. Home-made stocks from bones and root vegetables are economical. If you are using fresh marrow bones, first brown them in a hot oven for about an hour. Cook them gently in a heavy stew pan with plenty of water, vegetables and herbs, to make the stock. Always reheat a stock pot daily for 20–30 minutes to keep it fresh. Full-bodied soups make a good snack meal. Always skim excess fat from any soup before serving. When choosing starters, select lighter recipes or small salads (*see* Salad section).

Celery soup

1 head celery
2 beef or chicken stock cubes
420 ml ($\frac{3}{4}$ pt) hot water
1 dessertspoon skimmed milk powder

Suitable for slimmers   74 calories
Wash and scrub celery and chop coarsely. Dissolve stock cubes in hot water. Add celery and cook till tender, 30–40 minutes. Purée or beat till smooth. Return to pan and stir in skimmed milk powder and reheat.   *Serves 2.*

Marrow and tomato soup

2 chicken stock cubes
115 ml (4 fl. oz) hot water
335 ml (12 fl. oz) tomato juice
450 g (1 lb) marrow, peeled, cored and diced
1 chopped onion or 2 teaspoons onion flakes
salt, pepper
few drops sweetener (optional)

Suitable for slimmers   110 calories
Dissolve stock cubes in hot water; add the rest of the ingredients except salt, pepper and sweetener, and bring to the boil. Cover pan and simmer gently until marrow is cooked, about 20 minutes. Purée and return to the pan; season with salt, pepper and liquid sweetener, and reheat.   *Serves 2–3.*

Gazpacho (illustrated opposite)

1 clove garlic
1 large onion, chopped
900 g (2 lb) tomatoes, skinned
1 tablespoon cooking oil
280 ml (½ pt) beef stock
2 tablespoons vinegar
salt, pepper
pinch cayenne
1 teaspoon paprika
2 tablespoons chopped parsley

Garnish:
    green pepper, finely chopped
    cucumber, finely chopped

Suitable for slimmers   285 calories
Blend all ingredients until smooth, using mouli or electric liquidizer. Chill soup thoroughly; add a few ice cubes just before serving. Place vegetables for garnish in separate small bowls, so guests can help themselves.   Serves 4.

Kipper pâté (illustrated opposite)

2 boned kippers
85 g (3 oz) Panada white
sauce:
    20 g (¾ oz) flour
    20 g (¾ oz) polyunsaturated margarine
    85 ml (3 fl. oz) skimmed milk
30 g (1 oz) polyunsaturated margarine
1 dessertspoon lemon juice
cayenne
¼ teaspoon ground mace

Suitable for slimmers   697 calories
Place kippers head down in a jug and pour boiling water over them till covered. Leave to stand for 5 minutes. Pour off water, remove all skin and bones from kippers and allow to cool. Beat kippers till smooth and then blend in sauce, margarine, lemon juice, and season with cayenne and mace. Store in refrigerator. Serve with toast or use as a sandwich filling.   Serves 4.
    Suitable for slimmers if used as a snack meal.

Mushrooms with herbs (illustrated opposite)

225 g (8 oz) button mushrooms
2 tablespoons lemon juice
2 tablespoons oil
1 teaspoon milled coriander seeds
2 bay leaves
seasoning, freshly milled pepper

Suitable for slimmers   296 calories
Wash mushrooms. Trim stalks. Cut into thick slices. Place in dish with a squeeze of fresh lemon. Heat oil and coriander in heavy pan. Add mushrooms, bay leaves and seasoning. Cover pan and cook slowly for 5 minutes. Place in serving dish with bay leaves and pan juices. Add a further sprinkling of lemon juice and oil. Serve cold or hot.   Serves 4.
    Suitable for slimmers, if you use oil from day's ration.

Bortsch (illustrated opposite)

4 medium sized raw beetroot
2 beef stock cubes
1120 ml (2 pt) water
1 onion, stuck with cloves
1 level teaspoon caraway seeds
225 g (8 oz) shredded vegetables: leek,
   cabbage, celery
2 tablespoons oil
salt, pepper
pinch nutmeg
140 ml (¼ pt) low-fat natural yoghurt

470 calories
Peel and slice 3 beetroot; put into pan with beef-stock cubes, water, onion stuck with cloves and caraway seeds. Simmer gently for 1 hour or until colour has run from beetroot into stock. Sauté shredded vegetables and finely grated fourth beetroot in heated oil for 10–15 minutes. Strain stock, pressing out all juice from beetroot; return to pan. Add shredded vegetables and simmer until these are cooked. Season to taste and add nutmeg. Purée in liquidizer until smooth, or leave as a more chunky soup. Stir in yoghurt; reheat but do not boil. Garnish with a swirl of yoghurt. *Serves 4–6.*

Chilled cucumber and yoghurt soup (illustrated opposite)

2 large cucumbers
2 cloves garlic, crushed
1 teaspoon finely chopped mint
½ teaspoon grated lemon rind
1 tablespoon lemon juice
salt, pinch black pepper
1 tablespoon oil
225 g (8 oz) low-fat natural yoghurt
3 chicken stock cubes
560 ml (1 pt) hot water

Suitable for slimmers   244 calories
Peel and seed cucumbers; then grate them. Beat garlic, mint, lemon rind and juice, salt, pepper and oil into yoghurt until smooth. Add cucumber. Dissolve stock cubes in hot water, add to yoghurt mixture and chill thoroughly before serving. Garnish with thin circles of cucumber and chopped mint or parsley. *Serves 6.*

Country vegetable soup (illustrated opposite)

675–900 g (1½–2 lb) chopped root vegetables:
   potatoes, carrots, turnips, celery, etc.,
   including leek and onion
30 g (1 oz) polyunsaturated margarine
1120 ml (2 pt) water or meat stock
optional: 1 medium tin baked beans or
   115 g (4 oz) haricot beans, soaked
   overnight

777 calories
Toss chopped root vegetables in margarine. Add water or stock, and beans. Bring to the boil and cook gently for 45 minutes, if using baked beans, or 2 hours, if using haricot beans. Serve as a delightful chunky soup or liquidize for smooth thick soup. Garnish with parsley. *Serves 6.*

Cream of carrot soup

450 g (1 lb) carrots
2 medium potatoes
1 small onion
2 tablespoons corn oil
2 mixed herb stock cubes, dissolved in
    840 ml (1½ pt) hot water
140 ml (¼ pt) skimmed milk
chopped parsley

650 calories
Peel vegetables and chop. Heat oil in large pan and sauté vegetables for 2–3 minutes. Add stock, bring to boil and simmer gently for 1 hour. Rub through sieve or liquidize, add milk and reheat without boiling. Garnish with freshly chopped parsley.   *Serves 4.*

Leek and potato soup

450 g (1 lb) leeks
2 onions
450 g (1 lb) potatoes
55 g (2 oz) polyunsaturated margarine
140 ml (¼ pt) skimmed milk
1120 ml (2 pt) stock or use water and 2
    chicken stock cubes
salt and pepper
chopped parsley to garnish

938 calories
Trim the leeks, slice lengthwise through to the centre and wash thoroughly in cold water. Shred the leeks finely. Peel and chop onions. Melt margarine in a large pan, add sliced leeks and chopped onion and fry gently for about 10 minutes – do not brown. Add peeled and diced potatoes and cook for a further 5 minutes before adding the hot stock and seasoning. Bring to the boil and simmer for 30–40 minutes. Purée the soup, return to pan, add skimmed milk, reheat and serve hot garnished with chopped parsley. This may be served chilled.   *Serves 6.*

Cucumber soup

1 small cucumber
1 small onion
560 ml (1 pt) chicken stock or use 1 chicken
    stock cube to 560 ml (1 pt) water
pepper and salt to taste
pinch onion powder or onion salt
1 teaspoon lemon juice
2 level teaspoons cornflour

Suitable for slimmers   60 calories
Peel and thinly slice cucumber and onion. Bring stock to boil. Add sliced cucumber and onion and simmer gently about 5 minutes or until tender. Add seasonings and lemon juice. Mix cornflour smoothly with a little cold water, stir into soup and boil for 3 minutes, stirring constantly. For a smooth soup, put this through a sieve or liquidize. Serve hot or cold.   *Serves 2–3.*

Spinach soup

450 g (1 lb) fresh spinach or block of frozen
  spinach
15 g (½ oz) polyunsaturated margarine
1 onion, finely chopped
560–1120 ml (1–2 pt) chicken or beef stock,
  using stock cube

Suitable for slimmers   227 calories
Melt onion in margarine. Add fresh spinach. Cook
in covered pan for 3 minutes until leaves look
droopy. Add stock. Cook for further 10 minutes.
Purée in liquidizer or mouli. Add seasoning and
serve. (If using frozen spinach, add it when cooked
to melted onion. Top up with stock and cook 8–10
minutes.)   *Serves 4.*

Variation: *Watercress soup.* Use 2 bunches of
washed watercress instead of spinach and follow
same method for recipe.

Chicken broth

1 chicken carcass and giblets
1120–1680 ml (2–3 pt) water
1 onion
1 carrot
1 clove garlic (optional)
stick of celery or other chopped vegetables in
  season
salt, pepper
fresh chopped chives to garnish

Suitable for slimmers   60 calories
Cook chicken, vegetables and water gently for at
least 2 hours to reduce. Strain into bowl. Leave in
refrigerator. Remove fat when cool. Heat up stock
for broth, adding chopped chives.   *Serves 6.*
If stock has turned into a good jelly when cold,
this can be served as jellied consommé on warm
summer days.

Mulligatawny soup

2 tablespoons cooking oil
115 g (4 oz) onions, chopped
2 tablespoons plain flour
840 ml (1½ pt) stock
2 teaspoons curry powder
¼ teaspoon salt
115 g (4 oz) carrots, sliced
1 teaspoon lemon juice
2 teaspoons tomato purée
1 bay leaf
30 g (1 oz) Patna rice

1008 calories
Heat oil and fry onions without browning for 5 minutes. Add flour stirring well and cook gently without browning for 1 minute. Gradually add stock, stirring all the time until the mixture thickens. Add curry powder, salt, carrots, lemon juice, tomato purée and bay leaf. Simmer for 30–45 minutes or until vegetables are tender, then pass through a strainer or remove bay leaf and use an electric blender. Add rice and simmer for about 15 minutes or until the rice is tender. *Serves 4.*

Sherried onion consommé (illustrated on page 65)

4 medium onions, sliced
280 ml (½ pt) dry sherry
2 cloves garlic, crushed
black pepper
sprig parsley
2 beef stock cubes, dissolved in 840 ml (1½ pt) boiling water
1 tablespoon fresh orange juice
garnish: onion rings, orange peel

448 calories
Place onions, sherry, garlic, pepper, parsley and stock in pan. Bring to boil, simmer gently for 30 minutes or until onions are very soft. Strain liquid into bowl, add orange juice. To serve: garnish with onion rings or thin strips of orange peel. *Serves 6.*
Suitable for slimmers if sherry is omitted.

Onion soup

675 g (1½ lb) onions, thinly sliced
40 g (1½ oz) polyunsaturated margarine
1 tablespoon cooking oil
salt
¾ teaspoon sugar
40 g (1½ oz) flour
1820 ml (3¼ pt) brown beef stock

Suitable for slimmers   629 calories
Cook onions slowly in oil and margarine with salt and sugar. Add flour, and stir well. Add stock and simmer for 40 minutes. Serve with rounds of French bread. *Serves 8.*

Slimmers' soup

1400 ml (2½ pt) water or stock
675 g (1½ lb) cubed or thinly sliced
    vegetables in season (carrots, celery, leeks,
    mushrooms, onions, turnips, swedes,
    French beans, peas, celeriac – not   potatoes)
chopped parsley

Suitable for slimmers   128 calories
Prepare vegetables and cook for 30 minutes in liquid. Serve, garnished with chopped parsley. *Serves 6.*

Cream of mushroom soup

1 tablespoon finely chopped onion
55 g (2 oz) polyunsaturated margarine
225 g (8 oz) mushrooms
55 g (2 oz) flour
560 ml (1 pt) stock
560 ml (1 pt) skimmed milk
seasoning

890 calories
Cook the onion till soft in margarine. Add chopped mushrooms and sauté for 4–5 minutes. Add the flour and stir well, not browning. Add stock and milk gradually. Bring to the boil, stirring all the time. Season and cook for 5 minutes.   *Serves 4–5.*

Cock-a-leekie soup

1 chicken, about 1350 g (3 lb)
salt
6 peppercorns
6 leeks

Suitable for slimmers if used as a main course. 786 calories
Put the chicken and giblets in a large saucepan. Add salt and peppercorns and bring to the boil. Remove any scum from the surface and cook for 1½ hours with the lid on. Cut off the roots and trim coarse green from the leeks to within 5 cm (2 in) of the white stems. Slice lengthways through to the centre and wash thoroughly in cold water. Chop into 25 mm (1 in) pieces. Skim the soup again and add leeks. Simmer 30 minutes more. Remove chicken and giblets from the soup. Remove skin and bones; set aside best breast flesh for another recipe. Cut remaining meat into small pieces; add to soup; check seasoning. Garnish with chopped parsley. *Serves 6.*

Cream of celery soup

30 g (1 oz) polyunsaturated margarine
30 g (1 oz) flour
560 ml (1 pt) skimmed milk
seasoning
2 heads celery
560 ml (1 pt) stock or water

598 calories
Make a thin white sauce with margarine, flour and milk. Season well. Cook the scrubbed and chopped celery in stock or water until tender. Purée and combine with the white sauce, stirring well. *Serves 4–6.*

Cream of celery and artichoke soup

450 g (1 lb) Jerusalem artichokes
1 head celery
15 g (½ oz) polyunsaturated margarine
1400 ml (2½ pt) stock or water
seasoning

Suitable for slimmers   194 calories
Peel and slice artichokes; scrub and chop celery. Melt margarine and toss vegetables in this for 3–5 minutes. Add stock and seasoning and cook 30–40 minutes. Purée. Serve garnished with chopped parsley.   *Serves 6.*

Cream of chicken soup

1 tablespoon onion, minced or finely chopped
55 g (2 oz) polyunsaturated margarine
55 g (2 oz) flour
980 ml (1¾ pt) chicken stock
280 ml (½ pt) skimmed milk
seasoning
115 g (4 oz) cooked chicken, chopped

990 calories
Cook onion till soft in margarine. Blend in flour, but do not brown. Gradually stir in stock and skimmed milk. Bring to the boil and simmer for 5 minutes. Add seasoning and cooked chicken. Simmer for a further 5 minutes and serve garnished with chopped parsley.   *Serves 6.*

Lucy's soup

2 onions, thinly sliced
2 large potatoes, thinly sliced
280 ml (½ pt) water
115 g (4 oz) cottage cheese
sea salt
freshly milled pepper
280 ml (½ pt) skimmed milk

525 calories
Add onions, potatoes and cottage cheese to water in pan. Season and boil for 10 minutes until vegetables are cooked. Blend till smooth in liquidizer, or put through sieve. Add milk. Reheat gently, stirring. Serve, garnished with shredded cabbage or carrot. *Serves 4.*
Suitable for slimmers if used as a main course.

Scotch broth

225–450 g (½–1 lb) neck of lamb or mutton
1120 ml (2 pt) water
30 g (1 oz) barley
salt, pepper
bouquet garni
55 g (2 oz) turnip, diced
1 leek, sliced
2 carrots, diced
1 small carrot, grated

667–1080 calories
Wash meat. Trim off fat, and put meat into a large saucepan. Add water, salt and barley (washed); bring to the boil. Add pepper, bouquet garni and vegetables. Cook for 1½–2 hours, or until the meat is tender. Half an hour before serving add the grated carrot. When cooked, skim off excess fat and remove bouquet garni. Garnish with chopped parsley. This is a substantial soup which can be used as a main course. *Serves 4.*

Tomato soup

450 g (1 lb) tinned tomatoes or 450 g (1 lb)
    fresh tomatoes
700 ml (1¼ pt) stock and tomato liquid, mixed
piece of carrot and celery
1 small onion
15 g (½ oz) lean bacon
15 g (½ oz) polyunsaturated margarine
bay leaf, mace
15 g (½ oz) cornflour
140 ml (¼ pt) skimmed milk

389 calories
Strain liquid from tomatoes and add to stock to make 700 ml (1¼ pt). Fry chopped onion, celery, carrot and bacon in margarine. Add tomatoes and reduce heat for 3–5 minutes. Add stock, bay leaf and mace; simmer for 1 hour. Strain and purée tomatoes but not other vegetables. Thicken with cornflour dissolved in cold skimmed milk. Serve with fingers of thin toast. *Serves 4.*

Julienne soup

1 carrot
1 medium onion
¼ turnip
1 stick celery
15 g (½ oz) polyunsaturated margarine
seasoning
1120 ml (2 pt) chicken stock

Suitable for slimmers   116 calories
Clean and peel vegetables. Cut into matchstick shapes. Melt margarine in small pan. Gently fry vegetables for 5 minutes without browning. Drain on kitchen paper to remove fat. Add to hot chicken stock. Simmer for 15 minutes, skimming if necessary. *Serves 4.*

Hunter's soup

30 g (1 oz) polyunsaturated margarine
115 g (4 oz) raw lean ham or bacon, sliced
1 onion, sliced
1 carrot, sliced
1 or 2 sticks celery
1120 ml (2 pt) chicken stock
30 g (1 oz) cooked chicken or rabbit, chopped
seasoning, bouquet garni

814 calories
Melt margarine, add ham and chopped vegetables and soften. Add stock and cooked meat, seasoning and bouquet garni. Simmer gently for 1 hour. Skim any excess fat off top of soup before serving, garnish with chopped fresh herbs. A substantial soup good for using as a main course. *Serves 4.*

Suitable for slimmers if used as a main course.

Lentil soup

170 g (6 oz) lentils
1 large onion, chopped
30 g (1 oz) polyunsaturated margarine
1120 ml (2 pt) meat stock
*   or water and 2 stock cubes*
15 g (½ oz) cornflour
280 ml (½ pt) skimmed milk
chopped parsley

900 calories
Wash lentils. Soak overnight. Drain. Toss onion and lentils gently in melted margarine. Add stock and seasoning. Cover, bring to the boil and simmer, skimming occasionally, for 2 hours or until lentils are soft. Sieve and return to pan. Mix cornflour with a little milk. Add to soup with rest of milk. Bring to the boil, stirring. Serve garnished with parsley. *Serves 6.*

Scandinavian herrings (illustrated on page 64)

4 small rolled pickled herrings
1 red apple, sliced
½ red pepper, sliced
1 medium onion, cut into rings
115 g (4 oz) special mayonnaise (page 68)

680 calories
Toss apple, pepper and onion in mayonnaise. Place in serving dish with the herrings. *Serves 4.*

Smoky fish starter

450 g (1 lb) cooked smoked fish
140 ml (¼ pt) tomato juice
½ teaspoon Worcestershire sauce
½ teaspoon grated horseradish
½ teaspoon lemon juice
½ teaspoon vinegar
2 tablespoons chopped parsley

Suitable for slimmers   470 calories
Flake the fish. Mix with other ingredients and serve on shredded lettuce. *Serves 4.*

Easy eggs

6 eggs
115 g (4 oz) mushrooms
140 ml (¼ pt) skimmed milk
85–115 g (3–4 oz) cooked chicken
salt, pepper, paprika
chopped parsley

Suitable for slimmers   364 calories
Hard boil eggs; cool and shell. Cut in half lengthwise and remove yolks. Wash mushrooms and slice thinly into saucepan. Add milk and stew slowly for 15 minutes with pinch of salt. Slice chicken and add to mushrooms and liquid. Place in liquidizer and blend until smooth. Tip mixture into pudding basin. Add seasoning and mix well. Heap into egg whites. Garnish with a little paprika and serve cold on fingers of toast or bread. *Serves 4.*

Haddock relish

30 g (1 oz) polyunsaturated margarine
225 g (8 oz) fresh, tinned or bottled tomatoes
30 g (1 oz) flour
salt and pepper
pinch of dry mustard
280 ml (½ pt) skimmed milk
115–170 g (4–6 oz) flaked cooked smoked
   haddock
2 teaspoons parsley

Suitable for slimmers   570–628 calories
Melt margarine in a saucepan. Stir in tomatoes (sliced and skinned if fresh). Season and add a pinch of dry mustard. Stew gently until tender, then sprinkle in flour and cook for a minute or two. Add seasoning and skimmed milk gradually, stirring all the time, and cook for a few minutes. Add smoked haddock and heat through. Add chopped parsley and serve on hot toast.   *Serves 4.*

Soused herrings

2 small fresh herrings, filleted
140 ml (¼ pt) vinegar and water mixed
¼ teaspoon salt
1 blade mace
2 cloves
6 peppercorns

Suitable for slimmers   400 calories
Wash and clean herrings. Roll up, beginning at the tail end. Secure with a cocktail stick. Place in a small pie-dish with seasoning; cover with vinegar and water. Bake in a moderate oven, 325°F, 160°C, Mark 3, for ½–¾ hour.   *Serves 2.*

Rabbit and turkey terrine

450 g (1 lb) rabbit
thyme
4 peppercorns
2 bay leaves
560 ml (1 pt) stock or water
1 onion, sliced
½–1 clove garlic (optional)
salt and pepper
170 g (6 oz) cooked turkey
85 g (3 oz) Panada white sauce:
  20 g (¾ oz) flour
  20 g (¾ oz) polyunsaturated margarine
  85 ml (3 fl. oz) skimmed milk

Suitable for slimmers as a snack meal   1089 calories
Cook rabbit in stock with thyme, peppercorns, bay leaves and sliced onion until tender. Leave to cool. Mince the rabbit flesh, turkey and onion and beat well with a little of the stock, the Panada sauce, salt, pepper and crushed garlic. Cover and keep in the refrigerator. Serve with toasted brown bread. *Serves 8.*

Anchovies in a basket

2 cooked beetroot
1 large tin anchovies
2 hard-boiled egg whites
2 gherkins
seasoning
vinegar
2 tablespoons chopped fresh herbs

346 calories
Halve beetroot. Scoop out centres to make baskets. Soak in vinegar. Thinly slice anchovies, egg whites and gherkins. Mix. Season with salt, pepper and vinegar. Add herbs. Drain beetroot. Fill with anchovy mixture. Chill before serving. *Serves 4.*

Grapefruit starter

2 grapefruit
55 g (2 oz) polyunsaturated margarine
55 g (2 oz) demerara sugar

208 calories
Cut grapefruit in half, using a serrated knife. Loosen segments so grapefruit can be served in their skins and are easy to eat with a teaspoon. Divide margarine into 4, and place a knob on each grapefruit half. Sprinkle with sugar. Grill under medium heat for about 6 minutes. Serve hot. *Serves 4.*

Hot Main Dishes

Nourishing stew, simple roast or grill – whatever your favourite hot dish, the most important thing to remember is that it should contain as little fat as possible. Bread or kitchen paper are both useful for skimming fat off casseroles. Portions of dishes should not be too large. Make the most of white fish dishes because they contain useful protein. Less expensive fish like coley or hake are especially useful for made-up dishes. It is well worth experimenting with different herbs and seasonings to alter the flavour of homely recipes. These can often taste a little bland when cooked for diet purposes, so the seasonings and herbs are much needed to pep up the flavour. For additional information see the Introduction, page 9.

Rabbit casserole

1 rabbit
seasoned flour
85 ml (3 fl. oz) cooking oil
4 onions, sliced
parsley, thyme
salt, pepper
280 ml (½ pt) stock or mixed stock and red
 wine or cider

1490 calories
Joint rabbit and roll in seasoned flour. Brown joints quickly in hot oil. Cover with sliced onion and sprinkle with parsley, thyme, salt and pepper. Add stock and simmer in a tightly covered pan or casserole over a low heat, or in the oven at 325°F, 160°C, Mark 3, for 45 minutes to 1 hour. Skim off surplus fat before serving. *Serves 4.*

Rabbit pie

170 g (6 oz) flour
85 g (3 oz) polyunsaturated margarine
pinch salt
½ teaspoon baking powder
1 rabbit, jointed
seasoned flour
40 ml (1½ fl. oz) cooking oil
140 ml (¼ pt) stock
mixed herbs
grated rind of 1 lemon

2696 calories
Make shortcrust pastry by combining flour, margarine, salt and baking powder, adding water to mix. Dip rabbit joints in seasoned flour. Brown in hot oil and place in a pie dish with stock, mixed herbs and grated lemon rind. Roll out pastry to just larger than the pie dish. Cut off a strip of pastry, moisten edges of dish and place strip of pastry round. Moisten strip and place remaining pastry over pie. Trim off excess pastry. Make a hole in the top. Cook for 20 minutes at 400°F, 200°C, Mark 6, then for 1½ hours at 250°F, 120°C, Mark 2. *Serves 4–6.*

British fish pie

115–170 g (4–6 oz) flaked cooked white fish
2 hard-boiled egg whites, sliced
2 tomatoes, sliced
280 ml (½ pt) skimmed milk to make
   savoury parsley sauce
salt and pepper

Suitable for slimmers   315 calories
Place layers of sauce, flaked fish, tomato and egg in a fireproof dish. Finish with a layer of sauce. Brown in the oven for 30 minutes, 375°F, 190°C, Mark 5. Use sliced boiled potato in place of the parsley sauce as a variation.   *Serves 2.*

Russian fish pie

170 g (6 oz) flour
85 g (3 oz) polyunsaturated margarine
salt
½ teaspoon baking powder
225 g (8 oz) smoked haddock
140 ml (¼ pt) white sauce:
   15 g (½ oz) polyunsaturated margarine
   15 g (½ oz) flour
   140 ml (¼ pt) skimmed milk
1 teaspoon chopped parsley
dash lemon juice
salt, pepper

1861 calories
Make shortcrust pastry by combining flour, margarine, salt and baking powder, adding water to mix. Cut fish into small pieces and mix with sauce, parsley and lemon juice. Season with salt and pepper. Roll pastry out into a square. Trim and place mixture in centre. Brush edges of pastry with skimmed milk, fold corners to centre and seal. Decorate with pastry leaves, place on baking sheet and bake in a hot oven, 425°F, 220°C, Mark 7, for 40–45 minutes. (Cooked fish may be used.) *Serves 4.*

Salmon croquettes

1 tablespoon finely chopped onion
115 g (4 oz) polyunsaturated margarine
2 tablespoons plain flour
115 g (4 fl. oz) skimmed milk
220 g (7¾ oz) tin pink salmon or tuna, well
   drained and flaked
pepper
4 tablespoons fine dry breadcrumbs

1810 calories
Sauté onion in half margarine until just tender. Stir in flour and cook for 1 minute, stirring constantly. Blend in milk and cook, stirring, over medium heat until thick. Cool slightly. Stir in salmon and pepper. Add half breadcrumbs; mix thoroughly. Shape into 6 patties or logs and roll in remaining crumbs. Sauté in rest of margarine until evenly browned on all sides.   *Serves 3.*

Fish skillets

450 g (1 lb) fish fillets or steaks
3 tablespoons cooking oil
1 onion, chopped
3 tablespoons chopped green pepper (optional)
2 tablespoons chopped parsley
2 medium tomatoes, cut in pieces or 225 g
    (8 oz) tin tomatoes
4 tablespoons water or tomato juice
½ teaspoon salt, pepper
½ teaspoon basil or oregano

Suitable for slimmers   845 calories
If fish is frozen, thaw it enough to separate pieces. Heat oil in frying pan. Add onion, green pepper and parsley and cook until onion is golden, about 5 minutes. Add tomatoes, water or tomato juice, and seasonings; cook until tomatoes are soft. Add fish, cover and cook gently, about 10 minutes or until fish is done.   Serves 4.

Baked turbot in chives

Four 140–170 g (5–6 oz) turbot steaks
55 g (2 oz) polyunsaturated margarine
1 tablespoon lemon juice
1 dessertspoon chopped chives
salt, pepper

1508 calories
Brush fish with half-melted margarine and sprinkle with lemon juice. Arrange in a greased shallow baking dish and cover with foil. Bake for 30 minutes at 350°F, 180°C, Mark 4, until the fish flakes easily when tested with a fork. Combine remaining margarine with chopped chives and seasoning and heat slightly. Arrange fish on serving platter and pour over warm herb mixture. Garnish with parsley and slices of lemon.   Serves 4.

Broiled fish steaks

450 g (1 lb) fish steaks
2 teaspoons cooking oil per portion
salt, pepper, paprika
lemon juice
chopped parsley

Suitable for slimmers   650 calories
Arrange fish in preheated oiled baking tin. Add 2 teaspoons oil for each serving of fish. Sprinkle with salt, pepper and paprika. Bake at 500°F, 260°C, Mark 9, for about 15 minutes or until fish flakes easily when tested with a fork. Do not turn unless fish is very thick. Sprinkle with lemon juice and chopped parsley before serving.   Serves 4.

Oven-fried fish fillets

450 g (1 lb) fish fillets or *small whole fish*
115 g (4 oz) dry breadcrumbs
3 tablespoons French dressing
(2 parts cooking oil to 1 part vinegar/lemon/
lime juice)

Suitable for slimmers   1082 calories
If frozen fish is used, thaw it enough to separate pieces. Dip fish into well-seasoned French dressing, then into breadcrumbs. Arrange on an oiled baking sheet. Pour any remaining French dressing over fish. Bake at 500°F, 260°C, Mark 9 for 10–12 minutes, or until the fish flakes easily when tested with a fork. Serve with tossed mixed salad. *Serves 4.*

Fish cakes

115 g (4 oz) cooked white fish
115 g (4 oz) cold cooked potato
salt, pepper
1 teaspoon chopped parsley
juice of 1 lemon
flour for coating
cooking oil

732 calories
Flake fish, mash potato, mix together and season with salt, pepper, chopped parsley and lemon juice. Divide into equal portions. Shape into flat cakes with a little flour. Fry in oil slowly until golden brown. Drain on kitchen paper. Serve garnished with lemon and parsley.   *Serves 2.*

Mushroom cod

450 g (1 lb) cod fillet
115 g (4 oz) button mushrooms, sliced
1 small onion, chopped
55 g (2 oz) polyunsaturated margarine
skimmed milk
30 g (1 oz) plain flour
salt, pepper
chopped parsley
aluminium foil 45×45 cm (18×18 in)

Suitable for slimmers   766 calories
Skin fish; cut into 3 even-sized pieces; wash and dry. Season. Place in centre of greased foil on a baking sheet. Heat half margarine and cook mushrooms and onion gently until soft but not brown. Spoon on to fish. (Reserve any margarine in pan for sauce.) Fold over sides of foil, overlapping edges to form a loose parcel. Bake at 375°F, 190°C, Mark 5, for 35–40 minutes. Open foil and drain juices into a measuring jug; make up to 280 ml ($\frac{1}{2}$ pt) with skimmed milk. Melt rest of margarine, blend in flour and cook for 1 minute without browning. Add liquid, stirring. Bring to boil. Season. Pour sauce over fish and sprinkle with parsley.   *Serves 3.*

Parcel of plaice (illustrated opposite)

1 large plaice (or lemon sole), filleted
little polyunsaturated margarine
115 g (4 oz) mushrooms, thinly sliced
1 small onion, chopped
1 tomato, skinned and chopped
1 tablespoon cooking oil
salt, pepper
medium packet frozen peas
chopped parsley

Suitable for slimmers   707 calories
Lightly grease baking foil, lay in 2 fillets in the shape of fish. Put half mushrooms down centre of fish. Fry onion and tomato in oil until soft. Add to mushroom filling. Cover with remaining fillets and rest of mushrooms. Season. Fold over foil so that juices cannot escape; place in fireproof dish and bake at 300°F, 150°C, Mark 2, for 15–20 minutes. Open up foil carefully. Arrange edges to hold juices. Surround with cooked peas and garnish with finely chopped parsley.   *Serves 4.*

Spanish cod (illustrated opposite)

675 g (1½ lb) cod fillet
2 thick slices brown bread
40 g (1½ oz) polyunsaturated margarine
1 clove garlic, crushed
juice and grated rind of 1 orange
salt, pepper

1101 calories
Make bread into crumbs. Melt margarine in frying pan. Add crumbs, garlic and orange rind. Shake and stir until crumbs have absorbed all margarine. Place cod fillet in greased fireproof dish, season well with salt and pepper and cover with breadcrumbs and orange juice. Bake uncovered at 375°F, 190°C, Mark 5, for 20–30 minutes. Garnish with orange slices and watercress. Watercress salad and new potatoes are good accompaniments.   *Serves 3.*

American fish pie (illustrated opposite)

280 g (10 oz) cooked fish
280 ml (½ pt) white sauce:
   20 g (¾ oz) flour
   20 g (¾ oz) polyunsaturated margarine
   280 ml (½ pt) skimmed milk
1 teaspoon chopped parsley
squeeze lemon juice
salt, pepper
2–3 tomatoes
450 g (1 lb) cooked potatoes
30 g (1 oz) polyunsaturated margarine
skimmed milk

1285 calories
Remove all skin and bones from fish and mix with sauce. Add parsley, lemon juice and seasonings. Skin and slice tomatoes. Mash potatoes. Melt margarine in a pan; add potatoes, seasonings and skimmed milk; beat until soft and creamy. Put a layer of potato in a greased pie-dish and fill the dish with alternate layers of fish mixture and sliced tomatoes. Top with the rest of the potato and bake at 350°F, 180°C, Mark 4, until brown on top and well heated through, about ½ hour. *Serves 4.*

Kebabs (illustrated opposite)

Marinade:
  2 tablespoons cooking oil
  2 tablespoons dry sherry
  1 tablespoon vinegar
  salt, freshly ground pepper
  2 medium onions, sliced

335–395 g (12–14 oz) lean leg lamb, cubed
12 button mushrooms
slices green or red pepper, 12 small onions
cubes of pineapple, 4 tomatoes, halved

1100 calories
Place meat in a bowl and cover with marinade. Leave at least 1 hour – overnight if possible. Remove meat and press on 4 skewers alternating with mushrooms, green pepper, onion, cubes of pineapple and finishing each end with ½ tomato. Grill under hot grill for 15–20 minutes, turning occasionally and brushing with marinade. Serve on a bed of white or brown rice. *Serves 4.*

Goulash (illustrated opposite)

4 tablespoons cooking oil
675 g (1½ lb) lean chuck steak
450 g (1 lb) onions, sliced
2 tablespoons plain flour, 6 peppercorns
1 teaspoon capers, chopped
1 teaspoon parsley, chopped
1½ teaspoons paprika, 1 teaspoon salt
2 bay leaves, 1 teaspoon marjoram
140 ml (¼ pt) sherry (optional)
140 ml (¼ pt) stock
170 g (6 oz) spaghetti or noodles

2910 calories
Cut steak into 25 mm (1 in) cubes and lightly brown in half the oil. Remove from pan. Fry onions without browning for 5 minutes. Return steak to pan, stir in flour, bay leaves, peppercorns, capers, parsley, paprika, salt and marjoram. Add stock and sherry (or substitute equal quantity of stock), stirring well, and bring to boil, cover and simmer gently for 1½–2 hours or until the steak is tender. Drain well. Remove the bay leaves from the goulash and serve on a dish with the spaghetti or noodles as a border. Garnish with chopped chives or parsley and freshly ground pepper. *Serves 6.*

Burgundy pot roast (illustrated opposite)

3 tablespoons cooking oil
1125 (2½ lb) lean beef topside
3 tablespoons minced onion
2 cups sliced celery
1 clove garlic, finely chopped
420 ml (¾ pt) stock
85 g (3 oz) tomato purée
4 tablespoons red wine

Suitable for slimmers   2864 calories
Heat oil in a large heavy pan. Add beef and cook over medium heat, turning to brown on all sides. Drain off all oil. Add remaining ingredients and bring to boil; cover and continue cooking in moderate oven (350°F, 180°C, Mark 4) until tender, 2½–3 hours. Serve with boiled potatoes and fresh vegetables in season. The vegetables can be added to the casserole just before serving. The joint is removed to a separate meat plate for carving. Extra sauce may be served in a gravy boat. *Serves 8.*

Sukiyaki

675 g (1½ lb) lean rump steak
225 ml (8 fl. oz) stock
3 tablespoons soy sauce
½ teaspoon Aromat
4 tablespoons cooking oil
2 cups diagonally sliced celery
1½ medium onions, sliced
335 g (12 oz) mushrooms, sliced
335 g (12 oz) fresh spinach, cleaned

1900 calories

Slice meat, cutting across grain, into thin diagonal strips, 75 × 25 mm (3 × 1 in). Combine stock, soy sauce and Aromat. Heat 2 tablespoons of the oil in a large heavy pan; add half meat and brown, turning frequently. Add half soy sauce mixture, then push meat to one side of the pan. Add half of all the vegetables, except spinach, keeping each vegetable separate; cook, turning often, 3–4 minutes. Add half the spinach and cook 1–2 minutes longer. Place on serving dish. Serve at once with rice and sauce from pan. Cook remaining ingredients using the remaining 2 tablespoons of oil. Serve in the same way.   *Serves 6.*

Chilli con carne

1 tablespoon cooking oil
450 g (1 lb) minced lean beef
450 g (1 lb) onions, chopped
2 cloves garlic, crushed
335 g (12 oz) tomatoes, skinned and chopped
7–15 g (¼–½ oz) chilli powder, to taste
1 green pepper, sliced
115 g (4 oz) red kidney beans, soaked
¼ teaspoon salt
4 tablespoons water
2 tablespoons flour

1217 calories

Heat oil and fry minced beef and onions together with garlic until lightly browned. Add tomatoes, chilli powder, green pepper, red kidney beans, salt and three tablespoons of the water. Cover and simmer gently for approximately 45 minutes, stirring occasionally. Mix flour with the remaining water, pour into mixture and cook for 5 minutes. Serve with whole boiled potatoes.   *Serves 4.*

Beef patties

450 g (1 lb) lean minced beef
1 teaspoon lemon juice
grated rind of 1 medium lemon
55 g (2 oz) fine dry breadcrumbs
1 teaspoon salt
¼ teaspoon sage
¼ teaspoon ginger
½ cup beef stock or 1 stock cube, dissolved in 140 ml (¼ pt) boiling water

Suitable for slimmers   961 calories

Mix meat, lemon juice and rind, crumbs and seasonings together thoroughly. Add stock, mix thoroughly and let stand 15 minutes. Form into 4 meat patties, 75 mm (3 in) in diameter and 20 mm (¾ in) thick. Brush pan with oil. Pre-heat for about 3 minutes. Place patties in pan. Cook 7–8 minutes on each side. Mixture may also be made into a meat loaf if desired.   *Serves 4.*

Fried rice with beef

225 g (8 oz) lean rump steak, cut into 25mm
  (1-in) squares
1 tablespoon soy sauce
170 g (6 oz) Patna rice
4 tablespoons cooking oil
225 g (8 oz) onions, chopped
¼ medium cabbage, shredded
2 sticks celery, chopped
salt and pepper

1719 calories
Marinade steak in soy sauce for 20 minutes. Cook rice in plenty of boiling salted water until tender, approximately 15–20 minutes, rinse and drain. Heat 2 tablespoons of the oil and gently fry rice for 5 minutes, remove and keep warm. Heat remaining oil and fry onions, cabbage and celery with salt and pepper for 5 minutes. Add steak to vegetables and fry together for 5 minutes. Return rice to pan and cook all the ingredients together for 5 minutes, stirring continuously. Serve with chopped parsley, tomato and green pepper salad.   *Serves 4.*

Country mince

2 tablespoons cooking oil
450 g (1 lb) minced beef
225 g (8 oz) onions, sliced
225 g (8 oz) carrots, grated
2 tablespoons plain flour
salt, pepper
2 teaspoons mushroom ketchup
280 ml (½ pt) stock, boiling
85 g (3 oz) oatmeal, or porridge oats, lightly
  toasted

1766 calories
Heat oil and gently fry minced beef, onions and carrots until lightly browned. Stir in flour, cook for 2 minutes. Add salt, pepper, mushroom ketchup and stock, cover and simmer for 15 minutes. Stir in oatmeal, cover and simmer for 20 minutes, stirring occasionally. Serve with triangular snippets of toast, green peas and boiled potatoes.   *Serves 4.*

Three marinades for steaks

1. 4 tablespoons French dressing

2. 2 tablespoons cooking oil
  2 tablespoons vinegar
  1 teaspoon salt
  ½ teaspoon Worcestershire sauce
  ½ teaspoon garlic salt

3. 225 ml (8 fl. oz) red wine
  1 large onion, sliced
  1 teaspoon ginger
  1 lemon, sliced very thinly
  1 tablespoon salt
  12 peppercorns

These three marinades help to add extra flavouring to steaks. In each case, mix the various ingredients first. Pour over the meat. Let the meat then stand, covered, in a refrigerator overnight. Bring meat to room temperature before cooking and drain on kitchen paper. Then either grill or fry. These quantities are sufficient for 4–6 servings of meat.

Ox-tail stew

450 g (1 lb) ox-tail
30 g (1 oz) flour
½ tablespoon cooking oil
560 ml (1 pt) stock, salt
1 onion, 1 carrot
55 g (2 oz) turnip
mixed herbs or bouquet garni
blade of mace, 6 peppercorns

1165 calories
Trim all excess fat from ox-tail pieces. Blanch in boiling water. Dry ox-tail pieces on kitchen paper, dip in seasoned flour and brown in oil. Add stock and salt; bring to the boil and skim. Add vegetables, herbs, peppercorns and mace, and cook for 3–4 hours, stirring occasionally. A pressure cooker is a great help with this dish.　*Serves 4.*

Stuffed ox-heart

One 450 g (1 lb) ox-heart
30 g (1 oz) breadcrumbs
1 onion, chopped
salt, pepper
sage or parsley, thyme
2 cups thin brown gravy

Suitable for slimmers　720 calories
Trim the heart, cutting away sinews and fat to make a pocket. Wash well in cold salted water and dry. Season inside and out with pepper and salt. Mix breadcrumbs, onions, seasonings and herbs and use to stuff heart. Stitch or tie securely. Place in a deep casserole and pour over brown gravy. Cover and bake at 350°F, 180°C, Mark 4, until tender, about 3–4 hours. A pressure cooker considerably speeds up the cooking time. Some bought stuffing mixes are suitable, but check ingredients list.
Use only occasionally.　*Serves 4.*

French country beef stew

5 medium onions, sliced
2 tablespoons cooking oil
900 g (2 lb) topside or chuck steak
1½ tablespoons plain flour
pinch marjoram and thyme
pinch salt and pepper
8 tablespoons dry red wine with 4 tablespoons
　meat stock
or 12 tablespoons meat stock
225 g (8 oz) mushrooms, sliced
tomato juice may be added for extra flavour

Suitable for slimmers without wine　2343 calories.
Cut beef into 25 mm (1 in) cubes. Brown onions in oil in heavy frying pan. Remove onions to another dish. Roll meat in flour mixed with seasonings. Sauté beef in remaining oil until brown. Add wine and stock (or use all stock). Stir mixture well. Simmer as slowly as possible for 1½–2 hours. Add more wine and stock (2 parts wine to 1 part stock) as necessary to keep beef barely covered. Return onions to pan after meat mixture has cooked 1½–2 hours. Add mushrooms and stir. Cook 30 minutes longer. Add more wine and stock if necessary – sauce should be thick and dark. Serve with boiled new potatoes and peas.　*Serves 8.*

Carbonnade of lamb

450 g (1 lb) lean leg of lamb
15 g (½ oz) seasoned flour
30 g (1 oz) polyunsaturated margarine
2 tablespoons cooking oil
450 g (1 lb) onions, thinly sliced
1 clove garlic, crushed
560 ml (1 pt) brown ale
salt, pepper
1 tablespoon sherry (optional)

2055 calories

Cut lamb into 25 mm (1 in) cubes and coat with seasoned flour. Melt margarine with oil and add onions and garlic. Cover and fry gently for 15–20 minutes, stirring occasionally, until onions are completely soft. Remove onions and place in casserole. Fry lamb in remaining fat until brown on all sides. Add to onions with brown ale and a little salt and pepper. Cover and cook in a moderate oven, 350°F, 180°C, Mark 4, for 1½ hours. Before serving, check seasoning and add sherry. Serve with creamed or new potatoes and tossed green salad. *Serves 4.*

Lamb provençale

450 g (1 lb) lean leg of lamb, cooked
55 g (2 oz) polyunsaturated margarine
1 tablespoon cooking oil
2 medium onions, chopped
390 g (14 oz) tin tomatoes
1 tablespoon tomato purée
280 ml (½ pt) dry white wine
115 g (4 oz) mushrooms, sliced
1 large green pepper, seeded and sliced
salt, freshly ground black pepper

1970 calories

Cut lamb into 12 mm (½ in) cubes. Melt margarine with oil and add onions. Fry gently for about 10–15 minutes until soft but not brown. Stir in tomatoes, tomato purée and wine. Bring to the boil and add lamb. Simmer, covered, for 25 minutes. Add mushrooms and green pepper and cook for a further 15 minutes, stirring occasionally. Season with salt and pepper. Serve with creamed potatoes and haricot beans.   *Serves 6.*

Lamb à l'orange

1 small onion, very finely chopped
1 dessertspoon cooking oil
1 large orange
1 tablespoon redcurrant jelly
280 ml (½ pt) stock, skimmed
½ teaspoon dry mustard
½ teaspoon caster sugar
pinch cayenne pepper
1 tablespoon cornflour
335 g (12 oz) lean, cooked leg or shoulder of
    lamb

Suitable for slimmers   1183 calories
Fry onion gently in oil until soft but not brown. Grate orange rind; cut three fine slices from orange. Trim pith and reserve for garnish. Squeeze juice from remainder of orange and add to onion with rind, redcurrant jelly and stock. Bring to boil, reduce heat and cook, stirring, for 5 minutes. Blend mustard, sugar, pepper and cornflour together with 2 tablespoons cold water and stir into orange sauce. Slice lamb, add to sauce and bring to boil. Reduce heat and simmer for 15 minutes. Serve garnished with reserved orange slices.   *Serves 4.*

Ceylon curry

450 g (1 lb) lean cooked lamb
2 medium onions, finely chopped
1 tablespoon cooking oil
30 g (1 oz) polyunsaturated margarine
1 tablespoon curry powder
1 teaspoon curry paste
1 tablespoon tomato purée
½ teaspoon each ginger, cinnamon, salt
1 bay leaf
140 ml (¼ pt) stock, skimmed
115 g (4 oz) mushrooms, chopped
3 courgettes, 4 tomatoes
3 tablespoons sweet brown pickle or chutney

1868 calories
Cut lamb into 25 mm (1 in) cubes. Fry onion in oil and margarine until soft and golden brown. Add curry powder and curry paste and cook for 10 minutes more, stirring occasionally. Add tomato purée, ginger, cinnamon, salt and bay leaf and mix well. Stir in stock. Add mushrooms, courgettes (sliced), tomatoes (chopped) and pickle. Add lamb and bring to boil, stirring constantly. Cover and simmer for 45 minutes, stirring occasionally. Serve with pilau rice, i.e. rice flavoured with spices and cooked in stock.   *Serves 4.*

Lamb cutlets Maria

2 tablespoons cooking oil
3 lean lamb cutlets
280 ml (½ pt) sweet white wine
1 clove garlic, crushed
1½ tablespoons cornflour
juice of half a lemon
½ teaspoon rosemary
1 bay leaf
salt and pepper

1126 calories
Heat oil and lightly brown lamb cutlets on both sides. Add white wine, crushed garlic, lemon juice, rosemary, bay leaf, salt and pepper. Cover and simmer for 40 minutes. Place cutlets on serving dish and keep warm. Strain liquid, add cornflour and return to heat, stirring continuously until sauce thickens. Pour sauce over the cutlets. Garnish with wedges of lemon. Serve with carrots and potatoes. *Serves 3.*

Somerset lamb with rice

3 tablespoons cooking oil
225 g (8 oz) onions, chopped
675 g (1½ lb) lean leg of lamb
3 tablespoons plain flour
1 teaspoon salt
¼ teaspoon pepper
560 ml (1 pt) cider
225 g (8 oz) tomatoes, skinned and quartered
1 small packet frozen peas
170 g (6 oz) Patna rice
1 tablespoon chopped parsley

3554 calories
Cut lamb into 25 mm (1 in) cubes. Heat oil and fry onions and lamb for about 5 minutes or until lightly browned. Add flour, salt and pepper and cook gently for 1 minute. Gradually add cider stirring constantly until mixture thickens. Cover and simmer gently for approximately 45 minutes. Then add tomatoes and peas. Cover and simmer again until meat is tender. Meanwhile cook rice in plenty of boiling water until only just tender. Rinse in boiling water, drain and dry well. Serve lamb mixture sprinkled with parsley and bordered with rice. *Serves 6.*

Irish stew

450 g (1 lb) middle neck or breast of lamb
450 g (1 lb) potatoes
115 g (4 oz) onions
280 ml (½ pt) water or stock
salt, pepper

Suitable for slimmers   1080 calories
Trim fat off the meat and cut it into small pieces. Put into a casserole or stewpan and cover with hot water or stock. Add salt and bring to boil. Peel and slice onions. Wash and peel potatoes and cut one or two in half. Add onions and 1–2 sliced potatoes to the meat, season with pepper and simmer for 1½–2 hours. About 40 minutes before serving, add rest of the potatoes whole or cut in two. N.B. The remains of cooked lamb makes excellent Irish stew but should be thoroughly reheated only after the onions and potatoes are tender. Serve slimmers with ration of potatoes from the stew. *Serves 4.*

Haricot lamb

450 g (1 lb) lean mutton – middle neck or
  lean breast
1 tablespoon oil
30 g (1 oz) flour
560 ml (1 pt) stock or water
70 g (2½ oz) haricot beans
onion, sliced
carrot, turnip, celery, diced

1690 calories
Wash haricot beans and soak overnight. Trim fat off meat and cut into medium-sized pieces. Heat oil in a stewpan and brown the lamb quickly on both sides; lift out on to a plate. Fry onion till a golden-brown colour. Add stock or water, salt, pepper, meat and other vegetables including the haricot beans. Bring to the boil and simmer for 2 hours or cook in the oven, 325°F, 160°C, Mark 3. Baked beans may be used instead of haricot beans. *Serves 4.*

Lemon ginger chops

4 lean chump chops of lamb
Marinade:
    4 tablespoons cooking oil
    grated rind of 1 lemon
    2 tablespoons lemon juice
    1 tablespoon brown sugar
    1½ teaspoons ground ginger
    salt and pepper

1421 calories
Mix marinade ingredients together. Place chops in shallow dish and pour marinade over them. Leave for 2–3 hours, turning occasionally. Remove chops and place under hot grill. Cook for 15 minutes, turning chops occasionally and basting them with marinade. Serve with baked potatoes and mixed salad. *Serves 4.*

Shepherd's pie

225 g (8 oz) cold cooked meat or cooked mince
1 onion, chopped
½ tablespoon oil
7 g (¼ oz) flour
140 ml (¼ pt) stock or water, pepper and salt,
    mixed herbs (optional) to cover
450 g (1 lb) cooked potatoes
1 tablespoon skimmed milk
pepper and salt

Suitable for slimmers   940 calories
Heat oil in pan and fry onion, add flour and fry till brown. Add stock slowly, stirring well. Remove skin and gristle from cooked meat and chop or mince it. Add meat to gravy and season well. Pour into a pie dish. Mash potatoes, adding milk, pepper and salt, beating till smooth. Put potatoes evenly over the meat, decorate with a fork or knife and bake at 350°F, 180°C, Mark 4 for 18–20 minutes. Other vegetables may be added, e.g. cooked peas, baked beans, cooked celery, skinned tomatoes. *Serves 4.*

Mutton hot-pot

450 g (1 lb) stewing mutton, i.e. lean best
    end neck
450 g (1 lb) potatoes
115 g (4 oz) onions
115 g (4 oz) carrots
115 g (4 oz) celery
salt, pepper, parsley

1100 calories
Trim excess fat from meat. Peel and slice potatoes, slice onions and carrots, chop celery. Place a layer of potatoes in a casserole, season with salt and pepper. Add a layer of meat and a sprinkling of vegetables. Repeat layers, finishing with potatoes. Add water almost to cover. Cook, covered, over a very low heat for 2½ hours till the meat is tender. Skim off excess fat and serve sprinkled with parsley. *Serves 4.*

Roast veal with wine sauce

1350–2250 g (3–5 lb) piece of roasting veal
1 onion, chopped
1 carrot, grated
1 stalk celery, grated
4 tablespoons dry white wine
½ teaspoon salt
freshly ground pepper
½ teaspoon basil
¼ teaspoon garlic powder
½ teaspoon sugar

2604 calories
Heat oven to 450°F, 230°C, Mark 8. Place meat in oil in roasting pan. Bake for 20 minutes, turning frequently to brown all over. Spread vegetables over top of meat. Cover pan with foil. Reduce heat to 300°F, 150°C, Mark 2. Bake for 2 hours, or until meat is tender. Remove meat from pan and set aside to cool. Place meat juices in bowl and refrigerate. As soon as the juice is cool, skim fat off. Rub meat juices with vegetables through strainer and place in large pan. Add wine and seasonings to meat juice mixture. Slice veal thinly and add to mixture. Heat through and serve.   *Serves 6–8.*

Braised veal with herbs

900 g (2 lb) veal cutlets
2 tablespoons cooking oil
2 medium onions, cut in rings
1 clove garlic (optional)
¼ cup water
2 tablespoons lemon juice
½ teaspoon crushed oregano
1 teaspoon salt
2 tablespoons chopped parsley

1436 calories
Cut veal into serving pieces. Heat oil in large frying pan. Add veal; cook until brown on both sides. Remove from pan, add onions and garlic and cook until onions are tender. Remove garlic. Add veal, water, lemon juice, oregano and salt. Cover and simmer over low heat, turning meat occasionally until it is tender, about 30 minutes. Add extra water if necessary. Serve with chopped parsley.
Serves 6.

Breaded veal steaks

Four 115 g (4 oz) veal steaks, cubed
2 tablespoons fine dry breadcrumbs
salt, pepper
55 g (2 oz) polyunsaturated margarine

1051 calories
Dredge steak in crumbs seasoned with salt and pepper. Sauté slowly in margarine until browned on one side. Turn and brown on other side, allowing about 5-6 minutes per steak. Serve with new potatoes and fresh salad in season.   *Serves 4.*

Veal scallopini

1 small clove garlic, quartered
2 tablespoons cooking oil
4 small veal cutlets
1 tablespoon plain flour
½ teaspoon salt
few grains freshly milled pepper
few grains nutmeg
1 small onion, thinly sliced
4 tablespoons Sauternes or other dry wine (or part tomato juice)
115 g (4 oz) can mushrooms, drained
½ teaspoon paprika
1 tablespoon chopped parsley

1592 calories
Sauté garlic in oil over low heat for 5 minutes. Remove garlic and discard. Brown meat on both sides in oil over medium flame. Mix flour, salt, pepper and nutmeg; sprinkle over browned meat. Cover with onion and wine. Cover pan; simmer about 20 minutes turning meat several times. If liquid in pan simmers down, add a little more wine. Add sliced mushrooms, cover and continue cooking 8–10 minutes more. Serve on warm platter with sauce over meat. Sprinkle with paprika and parsley. Serve with plain boiled rice and green salad. *Serves 4.* 450 g (1 lb) thinly sliced veal steak cut into 75mm (3 in) squares may be used instead of veal cutlets.

Casserole of veal

450 g (1 lb) fillet of veal, cubed
1 onion, sliced
55 g (2 oz) chopped mushrooms
salt and pepper, chopped parsley
bouquet garni, 1 tablespoon lemon juice
560 ml (1 pt) fat-free stock or water
1–2 level tablespoons cornflour
skimmed milk

Suitable for slimmers   650 calories
Remove any fat from meat. Put meat, vegetables, flavourings and stock in casserole and cover. Simmer until meat is tender. Thicken liquid with a little cornflour blended with skimmed milk. Sprinkle with chopped parsley. Serve with boiled rice and courgettes.   *Serves 4.*

Veal pilaff

3 tablespoons cooking oil
450 g (1 lb) onions, chopped
450 g (1 lb) veal, diced
1 clove garlic, crushed
55 g (2 oz) almonds, split
55 g (2 oz) raisins
1 tablespoon preserved ginger, finely chopped
1 teaspoon salt, ¼ teaspoon pepper, bay leaf
560 ml (1 pt) stock
225 g (8 oz) Patna rice

2963 calories
Heat oil and fry onions and veal gently, without browning, for 5 minutes. Add garlic, almonds, raisins, preserved ginger, salt, pepper, bay leaf and stock. Bring to the boil, then cover and simmer for about 45 minutes to 1 hour, or until veal is cooked. Stir in rice, cover and continue cooking until rice is tender, about 20 minutes. Garnish with chopped parsley. Serve with tomato and onion salad. *Serves 4.*

Pork chops with plum sauce

3 tablespoons cooking oil
4 lean pork chops

Plum sauce:
450 g (1 lb) plums
140 ml (¼ pt) water
1 tablespoon plain flour
1½ tablespoons sugar
¼ teaspoon rosemary
salt and pepper

3244 calories
Stone plums and simmer in water until soft, then sieve. Heat oil and lightly brown each chop on both sides, reduce heat and fry for approximately 7 minutes on both sides. Drain well on kitchen paper and keep warm. Stir flour into remaining oil in pan, cook for 1 minute. Gradually add plum purée, stirring all the time. Add sugar, rosemary, salt and pepper and simmer for 3 minutes, serve with the chops. Serve with fried tomatoes, creamed potatoes and French beans. *Serves 4.*

Pork and cider casserole (illustrated on page 64)

3 tablespoons cooking oil
4 lean pork chops
30 g (1 oz) plain flour
560 ml (1 pt) cider
salt and pepper
225 g (8 oz) apples, peeled and sliced
225 g (8 oz) onions, sliced
225 g (8 oz) tomatoes, skinned and sliced
or 115 g (4 oz) cranberries

3486 calories
Heat oil and fry chops until lightly browned on both sides, then remove from pan. Mix flour with oil and cook for 1 minute. Pour in cider gradually and stir continuously until sauce thickens. Add pork chops, salt, pepper, apples, onions and tomatoes (or cranberries) to sauce, cover and simmer gently for 40 minutes. Serve with broccoli spears and creamed potatoes. *Serves 4.*

Apricot stuffed pork chops

4 lean pork chops
2 tablespoons cooking oil

Apricot stuffing:
115 g (4 oz) dried apricots soaked overnight
85 g (3 oz) white breadcrumbs
2 teaspoons sage
2 teaspoons parsley, chopped
salt and pepper

1900 calories
Slit each chop lengthwise from edge of meat to bone. Make stuffing by straining and chopping apricots and mixing them with other ingredients and then pressing together. Divide stuffing into four and fill each chop with mixture. Heat oil and lightly brown chops on both sides. Cover and fry gently for approximately 15 minutes. Drain well on kitchen paper. Garnish with parsley. Serve with creamed potatoes and spiced red cabbage. *Serves 4.*

Pork and mushrooms

1 tablespoon cooking oil
1 teaspoon salt
450 g (1 lb) lean pork shoulder, cut into
    25 mm (1 in) cubes
1 tablespoon soy sauce
¼ teaspoon pepper
280 ml (½ pt) boiling water
225 g (8 oz) mushrooms, quartered
1 tablespoon cornflour
2 tablespoons water

1573 calories
Heat oil with salt and gently fry pork until golden brown, approximately 8 minutes. Add soy sauce, pepper and boiling water, cover and simmer for 5 minutes. Add mushrooms and simmer for 5 minutes. Mix cornflour with water and pour into pork mixture, stirring continuously for 5 minutes. Garnish with chopped parsley and serve with boiled rice. *Serves 4.*

Casserole of belly of pork

450 g (1 lb) lean belly of pork
2 onions
1 carrot
1 stick celery
salt, pepper
mixed herbs
280 ml (½ pt) chicken stock (or use stock cube)
1 dessertspoon tomato purée or paste

Suitable for slimmers   665 calories
Trim off fat from the belly of pork. Place in a casserole and add chopped onions, celery, carrot, seasoning, tomato purée, herbs and stock. Cook for 1½–2 hours in a moderate oven, 350°F, 180°C, Mark 4. Skim off any surplus fat and serve. *Serves 4.*

Devilled chicken

4 chicken portions
seasoned flour
1 tablespoon cooking oil
225 g (8 oz) shallots or onions
mixed herbs
1 teaspoon curry powder
pinch cayenne
280 ml (½ pt) stock
55 g (2 oz) mushrooms

1352 calories
Roll chicken pieces in seasoned flour and fry in oil till golden brown. Add shallots or sliced onions and fry. Add mixed herbs, curry powder, cayenne and stock. Simmer for 30–40 minutes, add mushrooms and cook for a further 15 minutes.   *Serves 4.*

Chicken fricassée

560 ml (1 pt) Béchamel sauce:
  560 ml (1 pt) skimmed milk
  1 small carrot
  1 small onion
  1 small piece celery
  1 blade mace, 4 cloves
  6 white peppercorns
  55 g (2 oz) polyunsaturated margarine
  55 g (2 oz) flour
  salt
1 uncooked chicken or 4 chicken joints

1560 calories
Peel and cut vegetables into pieces and put in a pan with milk, salt, mace, peppercorns and cloves. Infuse for at least ½ hour, then strain. Melt margarine in a pan, add flour and cook well without browning. Add seasoned milk gradually, stirring all the time, and boil for 3–5 minutes. Cut chicken into joints and remove skin. Put in casserole and add hot sauce. Simmer gently for 1–1½ hours. With cooked chicken pieces the cooking time need only be ½ hour. Mushrooms may be added. *Serves 4–6.*

Coq au vin

4 tablespoons cooking oil
4 chicken joints
225 g (8 oz) onions, chopped
115 g (4 oz) lean bacon, diced
1 clove garlic, crushed
280 ml (½ pt) stock
¼ teaspoon mixed herbs
2 bay leaves
4 peppercorns
salt
560 ml (1 pt) red Burgundy
115 g (4 oz) mushrooms, halved
2 tablespoons plain flour

1782 calories
Heat 2 tablespoons oil and lightly brown chicken joints, onions and bacon with garlic. Add stock, herbs, bay leaves, peppercorns, salt and Burgundy, cover and simmer until chicken joints are cooked, about 30 minutes. Add mushrooms and simmer for 20 minutes. Remove chicken to a serving dish; strain sauce, placing onions, bacon and mushrooms on top of chicken; keep warm, reserve liquid. Heat remaining oil, add flour, stirring well, and cook for 1 minute without browning. Gradually add reserved liquid, stirring all the time. Simmer for 1 minute, then pour on top of chicken. Serve with creamed potatoes and broccoli spears. *Serves 4.*

Romany chicken

2 tablespoons cooking oil
4 chicken joints
335 g (12 oz) onions, sliced
390 g (14 oz) tin tomatoes
1 teaspoon salt
¼ teaspoon pepper, bay leaf
30 g (1 oz) flour
4 tablespoons liquid skimmed milk
1 teaspoon granulated sugar

Suitable for slimmers, if flour omitted   1100 calories
Heat oil and fry chicken joints gently until golden brown. Remove joints from pan and fry onions without browning for 10 minutes. Add tomatoes, salt, pepper and bay leaf. Place chicken joints in mixture, cover and simmer gently for about 30 minutes. Remove chicken joints to a serving dish and keep warm. Mix flour with milk and add to pan. Stir continuously until mixture thickens. Add sugar and cook for 5 minutes. Remove bay leaf, pour sauce over chicken joints and serve. *Serves 4.*

Chicken à la Sabra

1 cut-up frying chicken (about 900 g or 2 lb)
salt and pepper
paprika
1 large onion, sliced
3 tablespoons cooking oil
225 ml (8 fl. oz) orange juice
55 ml (2 fl. oz) white cooking wine
   (optional)
boiled rice
1 teaspoon curry powder
chopped mint or dill

2039 calories
Season chicken with spices. Brown onion and chicken in oil. Add orange juice and cook slowly, uncovered, for about 45 minutes, or until tender. Add wine and heat a few minutes. Taste and adjust seasoning. Serve on boiled rice, seasoned with curry powder. Top with mint or dill. For buffet service, remove bones from chicken after tender. Cut chicken into bite size pieces. Reheat in sauce and add wine. *Serves 4.*

Pineapple chicken cakes

170 g (6 oz) chicken, cooked and minced
1 small tin pineapple rings
55 g (2 oz) potatoes, boiled and mashed
or 2½ tablespoons instant potato flakes
55 g (2 oz) onions, finely chopped
grated rind of ½ lemon
salt and pepper
egg white and breadcrumbs, for coating
6 tablespoons cooking oil

1231 calories
Marinate cooked minced chicken in pineapple juice for 1 hour. Mix chicken and pineapple juice with potato, onion, lemon rind, salt and pepper. Divide mixture into four parts and form into round cakes placing pineapple rings in centre. Coat with egg white and breadcrumbs. Heat oil and fry cakes until evenly browned on both sides. Drain well on kitchen paper. *Serves 4.*

Breast of chicken sauté

2 large chicken breasts, cut in half
1½ tablespoons cooking oil
55 g (2 oz) chopped onions
115 g (4 oz) sliced mushrooms
4 tablespoons dry white wine
salt and pepper
white seedless grapes for garnish

Suitable for slimmers   1042 calories
Season chicken breasts with salt and pepper and sauté until lightly browned in the oil. Add onions, mushrooms and white wine. Cover and cook on low heat for about 30–40 minutes, or until chicken is tender. Serve with sauce from pan and garnish with white seedless grapes.   *Serves 4.*

Chicken with Amandine sauce

1 frying chicken (1125–1350 g or 2½–3 lb),
cut into pieces
55 g (2 oz) slivered almonds
2 tablespoons cooking oil
½ teaspoon salt
1 tablespoon lemon juice
½ teaspoon minced green onion
salt, pepper, powdered ginger

1424 calories
Pre-heat oven to 350°F, 180°C, Mark 3. Season chicken with salt, pepper and a pinch of powdered ginger. Place chicken, skin-side down, in baking dish and bake for about 40–60 minutes. Turn once during baking and baste either with juice in pan or with some fat-free chicken stock. If necessary for browning, raise temperature to 450°F, 230°C, Mark 8, for the last 10 minutes of cooking. Just before chicken is done prepare sauce. Sauté almonds in oil until lightly browned. Add lemon juice, salt and onion. Pour over chicken or serve separately. *Serves 4.*

Lemon chicken

1 frying chicken (1125–1350 g or 2½–3 lb),
cut into serving pieces
2 tablespoons cooking oil
3 tablespoons fresh lemon juice
rind of 1 lemon, grated
1 crushed clove garlic
½ teaspoon salt
dash of pepper
chopped parsley

Suitable for slimmers   944 calories
Arrange chicken in shallow casserole or baking dish. Pour lemon, garlic, salt, pepper and oil mixture over chicken. Cover and bake at 350°F, 180°C, Mark 4 until tender, about 45–50 minutes. Uncover casserole the last 10 minutes to allow chicken to brown. Baste occasionally during cooking. Before serving, sprinkle with chopped parsley.   *Serves 4.*

Chicken bake (illustrated opposite)

1 chicken, 1350–1575 g (3–3½ lb)
2 tablespoons seasoned flour
1–2 tablespoons cooking oil
1 clove garlic, crushed
1 medium onion, sliced
450 g (1 lb) carrots, sliced
450 g (1 lb) potatoes, sliced
450 g (1 lb) leeks, sliced
560 ml (1 pt) chicken stock, or water and
*   stock cube*
bay leaf, bouquet garni
1 tablespoon cornflour for thickening

Suitable for slimmers   1810 calories
Joint chicken. Remove fat. Roll in seasoned flour, brown quickly in oil. Place in stock, simmering gently. Soften vegetables in oil in covered pan with garlic. Add to casserole. Cook in oven at 275°F, 140°C, Mark 3, for 1½–2 hours. Skim off any fat, then thicken with cornflour mixed with ¼ cup cold water.   *Serves 6.* A meal in itself. Serve slimmers only allowed quantity of potatoes.

Chicken Jambalaya (illustrated opposite)

6 tablespoons cooking oil
4 chicken joints
225 g (8 oz) ham, diced
1 green pepper, chopped
225 g (8 oz) onions, chopped
1 clove garlic, crushed
170 g (6 oz) Patna rice
560 ml (1 pt) stock
salt and pepper
1 small packet frozen peas
chopped pimentoes for garnish

2437 calories
Heat the oil and lightly brown the chicken joints and ham. Add the green pepper, onions and garlic and fry without browning for 5 minutes. Add the rice, stock, salt and pepper, cover and simmer until cooked, approximately 20 minutes. Add the peas and simmer for 10 minutes. Serve with chopped pimentoes and tossed mixed salad as shown in dish at top right of picture.   *Serves 4.*

Chicken apricot (illustrated opposite)

4 chicken pieces, trimmed of fat
450 g (1 lb) tin apricots
or for slimmers: 1 lb apricots, poached in
*   water with artificial sweetener*
1 tablespoon Worcestershire sauce
juice of 1 lemon
1 tablespoon cornflour
seasoning

1170 calories   Slimmers' version 993 calories
Season chicken and put in baking dish. Mix juice from apricots with Worcestershire sauce and lemon juice. Cover with tight lid. Bake at 350°F, 180°C, Mark 4, for 50 minutes. Mix cornflour with 2 tablespoons cold water. Add to juice in baking dish. Arrange apricots round dish. Bake uncovered until gravy thickens and apricots are slightly browned, about 10–15 minutes.   *Serves 4.*

Aubergines with tomato sauce (illustrated opposite)

2 medium sized aubergines
30 g (1 oz) cornflour, seasoning
1 egg white, lightly beaten
30 g (1 oz) white breadcrumbs
oil for deep frying

Tomato sauce:
   15 ml (1 tablespoon) oil
   1 onion, finely chopped
   2 level tablespoons tomato purée
   420 g (15 oz) can tomatoes
   1 level teaspoon sugar
   ¼ level teaspoon basil, seasoning
   140 ml (¼ pt) red wine

Suitable for slimmers   755 calories
To make sauce: heat oil, add onion and fry until soft, without browning. Stir in tomato purée, tomatoes, seasoning, sugar, basil and red wine. Cover and simmer 20 minutes. Rub through sieve or liquidize. Reheat and serve separately. Peel aubergines and slice diagonally. Coat with cornflour, to which salt and pepper have been added. Dip in beaten egg white, drain and coat with breadcrumbs. Heat oil to 375°F, 190°C. Add aubergine slices and fry until browned. Drain on kitchen paper. Sprinkle with salt and pile into warmed serving dish. Serve with tomato sauce. *Serves 4.*

Stuffed peppers (illustrated opposite)

4 peppers
225 g (8 oz) minced raw beef
115 g (4 oz) mushrooms, sliced, or small
   whole button mushrooms
2 shallots, chopped
2 tablespoons oil
2 tomatoes, peeled and sliced
1 level tablespoon cornflour
140 ml (¼ pt) stock or water
pinch of thyme
seasoning

814 calories
Cut slice from stem end of each pepper. Carefully remove seeds and membrane from peppers. Blanch in boiling water for 5 minutes. Drain and cool. For filling: sauté beef, mushrooms and shallots in hot oil for a few minutes. Remove to basin and add tomatoes. Pour off oil from pan, leaving about 1 tablespoon. Add cornflour and mix well. Add stock, stir till boiling and boil for 1 minute. Pour over ingredients in basin, add thyme and correct the seasoning. Fill peppers, replace lids and bake at 350°F, 180°C, Mark 4, for 15–20 minutes. Lids can be removed before serving.   *Serves 4.*

Spiced red cabbage (illustrated opposite)

3 tablespoons cooking oil
450 g (1 lb) red cabbage, sliced
6 cloves, 1 bay leaf
1 small onion
2 tablespoons vinegar
1 tablespoon sugar
½ cinnamon stick, salt and pepper
280 ml (½ pt) stock
1 apple, peeled and diced

702 calories
Heat oil and fry cabbage without browning for 3 minutes. Stick cloves into onion and add to cabbage with bay leaf, vinegar, sugar, cinnamon stick, salt and pepper and simmer for 5 minutes. Add stock and apple, cover and simmer gently for 20 minutes. Remove the onion, bay leaf and cinnamon stick before serving. This dish is especially good with veal and pork casseroles.   *Serves 4.*

Cauliflower casserole

1 head cauliflower
3 tablespoons cooking oil
1 tablespoon chopped onion
3 tablespoons cornflour
3 cups skimmed milk
1 teaspoon salt
1½ teaspoons paprika
2 tablespoons chopped parsley
½ teaspoon Worcestershire sauce
2 tablespoons cooking oil
1 clove garlic
½ cup breadcrumbs

1539 calories
Separate cauliflower into flowerets and arrange in casserole dish. Cook until tender, about 5 minutes to keep the taste best and retain maximum vitamins. Heat 3 tablespoons oil in saucepan and fry onion. Blend in cornflour and stir in milk gradually until smooth and thick. Add parsley, salt, paprika and Worcestershire sauce and pour over the cooked cauliflower. Sprinkle breadcrumbs over top, either plain, or mixed with 2 tablespoons of oil heated with garlic, remove garlic. Good with roast dishes or ham.   *Serves 4.*

Stuffed marrow

1 marrow, medium size
Stuffing:
   225 g (8 oz) minced beef or minced cooked
   beef or lamb
   55 g (2 oz) dried breadcrumbs
   1 chopped onion
   2 chopped tomatoes
   1 tablespoon tomato sauce
   salt, pepper, mixed herbs

Suitable for slimmers   666 calories
Peel the marrow and cut in two lengthwise. Remove seeds. Parcook by boiling for 2 minutes or steaming for 5 minutes. Place on a fireproof dish. Mix all the stuffing ingredients together and fill the hollows in the marrow. Cover with foil or greased paper and bake in a moderate oven, 350°F, 180°C, Mark 4, till tender.   *Serves 4.* Minced ham, chopped corned beef or flaked tinned fish can be used instead of minced beef or lamb. Mushrooms and/or celery may be added to the mixture.

Braised courgettes

450 g (1 lb) courgettes
20 g (¾ oz) polyunsaturated margarine
salt and pepper, freshly ground
1 tablespoon hot water

201 calories
Wash and slice the courgettes. Place in a casserole dish. Dot with margarine and season with salt and plenty of pepper. Add water. Cook in a moderate oven, 325°F, 160°C, Mark 3, for 45 minutes to 1 hour.   *Serves 4.*

Tomato and marrow casserole

1 medium marrow
225 g (8 oz) tomatoes
2 large onions
seasoning and chopped parsley
½ clove garlic (optional), finely chopped or
   crushed

Suitable for slimmers   120 calories
Peel marrow, scoop out seeds and cut into slices.
Put alternate layers of sliced marrow, tomato and
onion into a greased casserole. Season each layer.
Bake in a moderate oven, 375°F, 190°C, Mark 4,
for 45 minutes or till tender. *Serves 4.*

Vegetable mix

675 g (1½ lb) diced vegetables, e.g. green beans,
   carrots, swedes, turnips, cauliflower, onion,
   sprouts, cabbage
tomato juice
salt, pepper
chopped parsley or chives

Suitable for slimmers   100–140 calories
Cook vegetables and drain. Season well and add
herbs. Bind with warmed tomato juice and serve.
Serves 4.

Tomato sauce

1 onion
¼ carrot
15 g (½ oz) lean bacon
15 g (½ oz) polyunsaturated margarine
4–5 tomatoes, skinned
or ½ tin tomatoes
or use tomato purée mixed with the stock
280 ml (½ pt) stock or liquid from tinned
   tomatoes
salt, pepper
pinch sugar
15 g (½ oz) cornflour if necessary

280–330 calories
Slice onion and carrot and cut bacon into small
pieces. Melt margarine, add carrot, onion and
bacon and fry lightly, then add the tomatoes.
Bruise tomatoes down with a spoon and cook for
4–5 minutes. Add stock, season with salt and
pepper; cook for 40–45 minutes, stirring occasionally. Sieve or liquidize. Reheat and add sugar and
cornflour dissolved in water if sauce is not thick
enough. *Serves 3–4.*

Ratatouille

2 medium onions, sliced
3 tablespoons oil
1 aubergine, sliced
4 tomatoes, skinned and chopped
1 green and/or red pepper, prepared and diced
2 courgettes, sliced
salt and black pepper

540 calories
This is basically a casserole of aubergines with other vegetables. The proportions can vary depending on availability and is even nice without the aubergines. Fry the sliced onions in oil till soft, add the other prepared vegetables, season and simmer gently in a closed pan for ¾–1 hour. *Serves 4–6.*

Sweet and sour beetroot

2 tablespoons cooking oil
2 tablespoons plain flour
1 tablespoon sugar
2 tablespoons vinegar
280 ml (½ pt) water
salt and pepper
675 g (1½ lb) beetroot, cooked and diced

940 calories
Heat oil, remove from heat and stir in flour. Add sugar and vinegar to water, blend into flour and oil, return to heat and bring to boil stirring all the time, then simmer for 3 minutes. Add salt, pepper and beetroot, cover and simmer gently for 5 minutes. This recipe goes well with lightly cooked lamb dishes. *Serves 4.*

Spiced gammon steaks

4 lean gammon steaks
whole cloves
1½ tablespoons mustard
4 tablespoons brown sugar
1 tablespoon cider
4 tablespoons cooking oil
1 small tin pineapple rings

2724 calories
Remove rind and fat from gammon steaks. Stick cloves into steaks. Mix mustard, brown sugar and cider together. Heat oil and fry pineapple rings for approximately 4 minutes, turning once, remove from pan and keep warm. Fry gammon steaks for 5 minutes on one side, turn and coat cooked side with mustard mixture and fry for a further 5 minutes. Serve immediately with pineapple rings, watercress, sauté potatoes and cauliflower. *Serves 4.*

Ham and pineapple hot-pot

2 tablespoons cooking oil
565 g (1¼ lb) lean cooked ham, diced
565 g (1¼ lb) cooked potatoes, sliced
450 g (1 lb) tin pineapple cubes
salt, pepper
1 tablespoon plain flour
1 small packet frozen peas, cooked
1½ teaspoons Worcestershire sauce
¼ teaspoon Tabasco sauce

1885 calories
Heat oil and gently fry ham and potatoes for 3 minutes. Make pineapple juice up to 280 ml (½ pt) with water and add to ham and potatoes. Add salt and pepper, cover and simmer for 15 minutes. Mix flour to smooth paste with 4 tablespoons of water and pour into ham mixture, stirring continuously; simmer for 3 minutes. Add pineapple cubes, peas, Worcestershire and Tabasco sauces, simmer for 5 minutes. Serve with creamed potatoes and carrots. *Serves 6.*

Ham risotto

3 tablespoons cooking oil
170 g (6 oz) gammon, diced, lean
225 g (8 oz) onions, finely chopped
115 g (4 oz) mushrooms, chopped
225 g (8 oz) tomatoes, skinned and chopped
170 g (6 oz) Patna rice
1 teaspoon tomato purée
420 ml (¾ pt) stock (fat removed)
salt, pepper

1911 calories
Heat oil and fry gammon and onions until tender but not brown. Add mushrooms, tomatoes and rice and fry gently for 5 minutes, stirring all the time. Mix tomato purée with stock, add salt and pepper and pour into mixture in pan. Bring to boil. Cover and simmer, stirring occasionally until rice is cooked and liquid absorbed, approximately 15 minutes. Serve with watercress salad. *Serves 4.*

Cold Main Dishes and Salads

For an easy summertime meal, there is little to compare with the flavour of home-cooked lean cold meats, a simple tossed salad and a potato in its jacket. Because salads play such a large part in the good hearted diet, it is useful to know a wide selection, ranging from the straightforward to the exotic. Meat loaves and galantines are a good way of making economical dishes more interesting. Although they are a little time-consuming to make, it is well worth while because you can ensure they contain all the correct ingredients and subtle flavourings. They also make a pleasant change from bought continental cold meats, which are not allowed because they contain too much fat.

Devilled beef rolls

2 tablespoons oil
1 onion, chopped
30 g (1 oz) cornflour
1 level teaspoon curry powder
1 beef stock cube
140 ml ($\frac{1}{4}$ pt) water
salt, pepper
1 tablespoon chutney
2 level tablespoons fresh breadcrumbs
*4 slices cooked beef, 40 g (1$\frac{1}{2}$ oz) each at the
   most*

860 calories
Heat oil and sauté onion until soft. Add cornflour, curry powder and beef stock cube. Gradually stir in water, bring to boil and cook for 1 minute, stirring all the time. Season and add chutney and breadcrumbs. Leave to cool. Spread mixture on slices of beef and roll up. Serve cold with salad. *Serves 4.*

Salmon loaf

Two 220 g (7$\frac{3}{4}$ oz) tins salmon
2 tablespoons skimmed milk
1 tablespoon grated onion
2 tablespoons lemon juice
$\frac{1}{2}$ teaspoon salt
pinch cayenne
2 tablespoons chopped green pepper
55 g (2 oz) chopped celery
$\frac{1}{2}$ cup dry biscuit crumbs
1 egg white

Suitable for slimmers   552 calories
Drain salmon and measure liquid; make up to 115 ml (4 fl. oz) with skimmed milk. Add onion, lemon juice, salt, cayenne, green pepper, celery, biscuit crumbs and egg white. Mix well and spoon into a greased loaf tin and bake at 350°F, 180°C, Mark 4, for 1 hour. Allow to cool for 5 minutes before removing from the tin.   *Serves 4.*

Salmon crunch

220 g (7¾ oz) tin red salmon
salt, pepper
pinch nutmeg
5 level tablespoons special mayonnaise
    (page 68)
1 small cucumber
2 tablespoons oil
2 slices white bread, diced
lettuce

988 calories
Flake salmon and remove any skin or bone. Add seasonings and mayonnaise and blend together. Dice half the cucumber, fold into salmon mixture and chill. Heat oil and fry bread until golden brown. Drain on kitchen paper. Fold into the salmon mixture and serve immediately on a bed of lettuce garnished with twists of cucumber.   Serves 4.

Yorkshire meat loaf

225 g (8 oz) stewing steak
115 g (4 oz) lean bacon
140 g (5 oz) white breadcrumbs
1 egg white
salt, pepper
pinch of sage and marjoram

1160 calories
Mince steak with bacon and mix with crumbs. Add seasonings and herbs and blend with egg white. Grease a pudding bowl, put in the mixture and spread smoothly on top. Cover with greased paper. Tie down and steam for 2½–3 hours. Cool in the bowl for a little, then turn out and leave till quite cold. Serve with salad. One tablespoon minced onion can be used instead of the herbs if preferred. Serves 6.

Ham ring mould

3 teaspoons gelatine
¼ cup hot water
450 g (16 oz) tin tomato juice
2 teaspoons sugar
salt, pepper
1 cup diced celery
1 cup grated carrot
225 g (8 oz) lean, diced ham

Suitable for slimmers   408 calories
Dissolve gelatine in hot water, add to tomato juice, add sugar, salt and pepper to taste. Leave to thicken, then stir in carrot and celery. Place in a ring mould. Chill. Unmould on shredded lettuce, fill centre with ham. Garnish with salad in season. Serves 3–4.

Salmon mousse (illustrated opposite)

Two 220 g (7¾ oz) tins red salmon (or tuna
  fish)
55 g (2 oz) fresh breadcrumbs
140 ml (¼ pt) skimmed milk
1 heaped tablespoon minced (or chopped)
  parsley
½ teaspoon salt
dash cayenne
1 dessertspoon lemon juice
1 tablespoon Worcestershire sauce
15 g (½ oz) gelatine
2 egg whites
capers for garnish

Suitable for slimmers   741 calories
Drain salmon into large basin, reserving juice.
Remove any skin and bone; flake flesh. Put milk
and breadcrumbs into small pan and add salmon
juice. Cook mixture over low heat, stirring, for
about 5 minutes. Add to salmon with lemon juice,
seasoning and minced parsley. Melt gelatine in a
little warm water; add to mixture. Whisk egg whites
till very stiff and fold into mixture. Oil a basin or
ring mould, fill with mixture and cover top with a
round of greaseproof paper. Set in a pan with hot
water quarter-way up the side of the basin. Bake in
pre-heated oven, 350F,° 180°C, Mark 4, for 40-45
minutes. A ring mould looks attractive as the centre
can be filled with capers or parsley sauce, or sauce
can be served separately.   Serves 4–6.

Quick brawn (illustrated opposite)

3 teaspoons gelatine
¼ cup hot water
280 ml (½ pt) low-fat stock, gravy or soup
3 cups lean, cooked meat, cut in small pieces
salt, pepper, nutmeg
2 hard-boiled egg whites

Suitable for slimmers   492 calories
Dissolve gelatine in hot water, add to stock. Season
meat with salt, pepper and nutmeg. Pack in basin
or loaf tin with slices of hard-boiled egg whites. Add
gelatine mixture. Leave to set in refrigerator or cool
place. Serve in slices with salads.   Serves 6.

Tomato meat loaf (illustrated opposite)

450 g (1 lb) lean minced beef
115 g (4 oz) breadcrumbs
225 g (8 oz) grated carrot
1 teaspoon prepared mustard
1 tablespoon Worcestershire sauce
2 tablespoons tomato sauce
salt, pepper
1 egg white

Suitable for slimmers   1171 calories
Mix all ingredients together. Line a loaf or 17 cm
(7 in) cake tin with greased greaseproof paper.
Cook 1½ hours at 300°F, 150°C, Mark 3, standing
in a tin of water in the oven. The water should be
half-way up the outside of the tin. Leave till cold.
Serve with tomato quarters and mixed salad.
Serves 8.

Summer rice salad (illustrated opposite)

225 g (8 oz) cold cooked rice
450 g (1 lb) chopped cooked chicken and/or
  ham
¼ cucumber, sliced
1 medium onion, chopped finely
1 green pepper, cut in strips
small tin sweetcorn, drained
2 tablespoons French dressing
small carton low-fat natural yoghurt
juice of lemon to taste
chopped chives to garnish
freshly ground pepper

Suitable for slimmers   1451 calories
Combine rice with meat and salad vegetables. Mix French dressing with yoghurt and lemon juice to taste. Mix everything thoroughly. Spoon on to serving dish. Garnish with chives and freshly ground pepper.   *Serves 8.*

A radish and curly endive salad, pictured top left, is a good accompaniment that turns this into a delicious main course for a summer supper party.

New Zealand fish salad (illustrated opposite)

4 fish steaks, preferably salmon
225 g (8 oz) new potatoes
115 g (4 oz) packet frozen French beans
1 lettuce
225 g (8 oz) shredded carrots
½ sliced cucumber
8 slices orange
115 ml (4 fl. oz) French dressing

With dressing: 1764 calories   Without dressing: 1226 calories
Cook potatoes and beans and leave to cool. Grill fish steaks and cool. Line serving dish with lettuce leaves. Fill with sliced cold potatoes, beans, carrots, and cucumber. Place fish in centre. Decorate with orange. Sprinkle with dressing and serve.   *Serves 4.*

Piquant roast beef salad (illustrated opposite)

170–225 g (6–8 oz) cold roast beef
3 tablespoons oil
1 tablespoon wine vinegar
1½ level teaspoons dry mustard
1 teaspoon anchovy essence
2 teaspoons chopped capers
1 level tablespoon chopped chives
1 level tablespoon chopped parsley
black pepper

Suitable for slimmers   822–964 calories
Cut beef into small strips. Blend oil, vinegar, mustard and anchovy essence thoroughly. Add capers, chives, parsley and pepper. Marinate meat in this dressing for about 1 hour. Garnish with extra chopped parsley. Serve with green salad. *Serves 4.*

Low cholesterol mayonnaise

1 dessertspoon cornflour
170 ml (6 fl. oz) skimmed milk
½ teaspoon salt
2 teaspoons sugar
1 teaspoon dry mustard
½ teaspoon paprika
4 tablespoons oil
4 tablespoons vinegar or lemon juice

689 calories
Mix cornflour to a paste with milk. Cook until thickened. Place in basin with salt, sugar, mustard and paprika. Beat well until smooth. Add a tablespoon of oil and a tablespoon of vinegar, beating constantly. Continue adding alternate tablespoons of oil and vinegar until mixture is complete and well blended.

Summer mould

1 chicken stock cube
280 ml (½ pt) hot water
1 level tablespoon gelatine
¼ teaspoon Tabasco sauce
3 tablespoons lemon juice
5 tablespoons special mayonnaise (page 68)
¼ small onion, finely chopped
2–3 sticks celery, chopped
1 red skinned apple, chopped
55 g (2 oz) cooked peas
225–335 g (8–12 oz) cooked chicken, diced
watercress, slices of red apple

With mayonnaise: 783 calories   Without mayonnaise: 551 calories
Add hot water to chicken stock cube and stir well. Dissolve gelatine in hot stock. Stir in Tabasco sauce and lemon juice. Leave to cool, but not set. Gradually stir in mayonnaise. When setting add onion, celery, apple, peas and chicken. Turn into wetted 16 cm (6½ in) ring mould and leave to set. Turn out on serving dish. Garnish with slices of apple and watercress. *Serves 4–6.* Suitable for slimmers if mayonnaise is left out.

Salmon or chicken mould

280 ml (½ pt) aspic jelly made up
½ cucumber, thinly sliced
2 hard-boiled egg whites, sliced
220 g (7¾ oz) tin salmon
    or similar amount finely chopped cooked chicken
225 g (8 oz) carton cottage cheese
2 tablespoons special mayonnaise (page 68)
salt and pepper
1 tablespoon chopped gherkin

Suitable for slimmers   656 calories
Pour 6 mm (¼ in) layer of aspic jelly into 840 ml (1½ pt) oval dish. Chill. When set arrange slices of cucumber and egg white on base. Chill. Pour another 6 mm (¼ in) layer of jelly on top. Chill. Mix together remaining aspic jelly, chopped egg white, flaked salmon, cottage cheese, mayonnaise, seasoning and chopped gherkin. Turn into dish and chill. Turn out on to a plate and serve, surrounded with shredded lettuce.   *Serves 4.*

Chicken galantine

280 ml (½ pt) hot stock
salt and freshly ground pepper
parsley, thyme
½ bay leaf
7 g (¼ oz) gelatine
2 tablespoons cold water
slices of cucumber
55 g (2 oz) cooked peas
335 g (12 oz) cooked chicken, turkey or
  rabbit
55 g (2 oz) minced ham

Suitable for slimmers   850 calories
Infuse herbs and bay leaf in seasoned stock for 10 minutes. Add gelatine to the cold water; stand for 5–10 minutes, then dissolve over hot water. Strain stock. Add dissolved gelatine. Arrange cucumber slices and peas in base of mould or serving dish. Add chicken, cut into small pieces, and minced ham. Pour over jelly mixture when it begins to thicken. Set in refrigerator. Serve with tossed salad. *Serves 6.*

This is an attractive-looking dish when made in a ring mould.

Meat and tomato brawn

15 g (½ oz) gelatine
140 ml (¼ pt) cold water
195 ml (⅓ pt) tomato purée
  (small tin of purée can be diluted with
  added water)
1 onion, sliced
2 cloves
pinch mixed herbs
salt, pepper
335 g (12 oz) cooked meat, minced or finely
  chopped

Suitable for slimmers   830 calories
Add gelatine to cold water in small bowl. Leave to stand for 5–10 minutes. Stand bowl in pan of hot water until gelatine dissolves. In separate pan boil tomato purée, onion, cloves and herbs. Add dissolved gelatine and seasoning. Strain. Add meat. Place in shallow dish and set in refrigerator. Serve with tossed salad.   *Serves 6.*

Vegetable vinaigrette

450 g (1 lb) mixed vegetables: celery, leeks,
  beans, carrots, cucumber, mushrooms, etc.
1 chicken stock cube
420 ml (¾ pt) boiling water

Vinaigrette dressing:
  2 tablespoons vinegar
  ½ level teaspoon salt, pepper
  ¼ level teaspoon dry mustard
  little finely chopped parsley
  4 tablespoons corn oil

Suitable for slimmers   610 calories
Prepare vegetables, cut into dice, and poach until tender in the stock made by dissolving chicken stock cube in boiling water. Do not overcook vegetables as they should retain their shape. Strain and leave to cool, then pour the dressing over. To make dressing: mix vinegar with seasonings, add oil and parsley and whisk with fork.   Serves 4.

American salad

1 lettuce
225 g (8 oz) cottage cheese

Dressing:
  2 tablespoons oil
  1 tablespoon vinegar
  ¼ level teaspoon salt
  1 level teaspoon sugar

A few of these for garnish:
  pineapple chunks, slices of peach, apple
  radishes, watercress, walnuts, chopped

Suitable for slimmers   about 603 calories
Put dressing ingredients in screw-top jar and shake well. Toss lettuce leaves in a little dressing and arrange on 4 individual plates. Place cottage cheese in centre of each and garnish with fruit and vegetables. Sprinkle with chopped walnuts and serve remaining dressing separately.   Serves 4.

Apple and olive salad

2 eating apples
1 tablespoon lemon juice
10–12 stuffed olives
6 radishes, sliced
1 small green pepper
lettuce

French dressing:
  2 tablespoons oil
  1 tablespoon vinegar
  pinch sugar, salt, pepper

Suitable for slimmers   450 calories
Mix ingredients for French dresing well together. Core and finely chop apples. Toss in lemon juice; add stuffed olives, radishes, seeded and finely chopped green pepper. Toss all ingredients in French dressing. Serve on a bed of lettuce. Serves 3–4.

Courgette salad

1 lettuce, Cos or Webbs Wonderful
4 small courgettes
1 small onion
2 tomatoes
1 green pepper
1 clove garlic (optional)
salt, pepper
4 tablespoons French dressing or wine vinegar

With French dressing: 594 calories   Suitable for slimmers with wine vinegar: 76 calories
Wash lettuce and tear up into small pieces. Slice the courgettes, onion, green pepper and cut tomato into wedges. Rub the serving bowl with garlic. Toss all the vegetables in the French dressing. Season with salt and pepper and pile into serving bowl. *Serves 4.*

Carrot and horseradish salad

450 g (1 lb) carrots
1 eating apple
1 level tablespoon horseradish relish or fresh grated horseradish

Dressing:
2 level tablespoons corn oil
2 level tablespoons white wine vinegar
salt and pepper
½ level teaspoon caster sugar

sprigs of parsley for garnish

Suitable for slimmers   408 calories
Peel and grate carrots. Peel, core and grate apple. Mix together carrot, apple and horseradish and put into salad bowl. To make dressing: mix together corn oil, vinegar, salt, pepper and sugar. Pour over the salad. Garnish with sprigs of parsley. *Serves 3–4.*

Chicken Mexicana salad

4 tomatoes
1 green pepper, deseeded and chopped
170 g (6 oz) long grain rice, cooked and drained
225 g (8 oz) cooked chicken, sliced

French dressing:
2 tablespoons corn oil
1 tablespoon vinegar
pinch sugar, salt and pepper

1397 calories
Mix ingredients for dressing well together. Chop tomatoes, leaving half for garnish. Mix tomatoes and pepper together and toss in French dressing. Lay cooked rice round edge of dish, then tomatoes and peppers. Lay sliced chicken in the centre and garnish with tomato half.   *Serves 4.*

Cucumber salad

450 g (1 lb) brussels sprouts
1 small cucumber
1 carton low fat natural yoghurt
1 tablespoon special mayonnaise (page 68)
1 tablespoon lemon juice
salt and pepper

Suitable for slimmers   250 calories
Remove damaged leaves from sprouts. Wash, dry and shred remaining leaves finely. Arrange in serving dish. Peel cucumber and dice finely. Combine yoghurt with mayonnaise, lemon juice and seasoning to taste. Add cucumber to dressing and pile in serving dish. Garnish with sprinkling of red pepper.   *Serves 4.*

Pasta salad

170 g (6 oz) small pasta shapes
1 small packet mixed frozen vegetables
½ cucumber
2 tomatoes, skinned and seeded
4 tablespoons French dressing

935 calories
Cook pasta as directed on packet in boiling salted water until just tender. Add mixed vegetables to pan of lightly salted boiling water, simmer for 2 minutes and drain. Allow to cool. Dice cucumber. Mix together cooked pasta, mixed vegetables, cucumber and tomato. Toss in French dressing before serving.   *Serves 4.*

Salad Romano

335 g (12 oz) long grain rice
220 g (7¾ oz) tin tuna fish
115 g (4 oz) cooked peas
1 red pepper, chopped
2–3 gherkins, sliced
6–8 anchovy fillets, drained well

Dressing:
   3 tablespoons corn oil
   1 tablespoon wine vinegar
   1 clove garlic, crushed
   ¼ level teaspoon salt
   1 level teaspoon sugar

2054 calories
Put all salad dressing ingredients in screw-top jar and shake well. Chill. Cook rice in boiling salted water until tender. Drain rice and rinse with hot water. Place in colander over simmering water for 5 minutes to remove moisture. Cool rice. Combine rice, flaked tuna fish, cooked peas, pepper and gherkins and decorate with anchovy fillets.
Serves 6.

Grapefruit salad

2 fresh grapefruit
115 g (4 oz) cottage cheese
chives or spring onions, chopped
55 g (2 oz) mandarin orange sections
½ dessert apple, chopped
1 stick celery, diced
½ green pepper, chopped

Dressing:
3 tablespoons corn oil
1 tablespoon vinegar
¼ level teaspoon salt
1 level teaspoon sugar

Suitable for slimmers. 633 calories
Put all salad dressing ingredients in screw-top jar and shake well. To assemble the salad: cut each grapefruit in half then carefully remove grapefuit segments, cutting away pith. Remove any pith and skin from centre of each half. Combine cottage cheese and chopped chives and place some in each grapefruit half. Combine grapefruit segments, mandarins, chopped apple, celery and pepper and toss all together in the prepared chilled dressing. Arrange this mixture in grapefruit halves and serve with extra salad as liked. *Serves 4.*

Tomato and orange salad

3 large oranges
450 g (1 lb) tomatoes
1 carton low-fat natural yoghurt
2 tablespoons French dressing
seasoning

Suitable for slimmers 434 calories
Peel oranges, cut into segments removing skin from each. Blanch tomatoes and remove skin. Cut into wedges. Arrange orange and tomato alternately in serving dish. Mix yoghurt, dressing and seasoning together and pour over salad. Chill before serving. *Serves 4.*

Cauliflower salad (illustrated opposite)

1 medium cauliflower head
3 sticks celery, sliced
115 g (4 oz) radishes, sliced (optional)
1 crisp apple, peeled and sliced
2 spring onions, sliced
1 red pepper, seeded and sliced
3 tablespoons chopped fresh herbs
1 cup French dressing, seasoned with crushed
    garlic
celery leaves for garnish

Suitable for slimmers   1071 calories
Wash cauliflower and divide into flowerets. Mix cauliflower with celery, radishes, apple, spring onions, sliced pepper and herbs, and chill in refrigerator. Toss in dressing. Garnish with celery leaves. *Serves 6.*

Use cauliflower and celery as basis for this salad and vary other ingredients according to season.

Tomato and anchovy salad (illustrated opposite)

4 large tomatoes
1 medium onion
large tin anchovy fillets
chopped fresh chives or spring onion tops
4 tablespoons oil
2 tablespoons wine vinegar
clove of garlic, crushed (optional)
salt and freshly ground pepper

1096 calories
Peel and thinly slice tomatoes and onion, and arrange on plate. Decorate with the anchovies. Sprinkle with dressing made from the oil, vinegar, garlic and seasoning. Garnish with chives.   *Serves 4.*

Spinach and bacon salad (illustrated opposite)

450 g (1 lb) fresh spinach
2 lettuce hearts
170 g (6 oz) lean bacon
225 g (8 oz) cottage cheese

Dressing:
    1 teaspoon dry mustard
    4 tablespoons cooking oil
    2 tablespoons wine vinegar
    salt and freshly ground pepper

2058 calories
Remove spinach stems. Wash spinach and lettuce leaves and tear or chop finely. Combine together. Fry bacon. When crisp, cool on kitchen paper to absorb excess fat. Crumble bacon and add to spinach. Mix dressing and use half to toss salad. Mix remaining dressing with cheese and place on serving dish. Surround with spinach mixture. *Serves 4.*

French beans vinaigrette (illustrated opposite)

1 beef stock cube
420 ml (¾ pt) boiling water
225 g (½ lb) French beans, shredded

Vinaigrette dressing:
  3 tablespoons corn oil
  1 tablespoon vinegar
  ¼ level teaspoon salt
  pepper
  pinch dry mustard
  little finely chopped parsley

Garnish (optional):
  few radish slices
  few mushroom slices

Suitable for slimmers   470 calories
Dissolve beef cube in boiling water then simmer shredded beans in this stock until tender. Drain and leave to cool. For dressing: put oil, vinegar and seasonings in screw top jar and shake well, then add chopped parsley. Chill and shake again before using. Slice mushrooms and sprinkle with a little dressing. Pour dressing over and mix well with beans just before serving. Garnish with mushrooms and sliced radishes.   *Serves 4.*

Coleslaw and fruit salad (illustrated opposite)

225 g (8 oz) Dutch cabbage, finely chopped
  and washed
55 g (2 oz) carrots, grated
1 red-skinned sweet apple, sliced
1 orange, segmented
4 tablespoons special mayonnaise (page 68)
a few walnuts for garnish (optional)

With mayonnaise: 344 calories   Without mayonnaise: 148 calories
Mix cabbage, carrot, apple and orange segments together. Toss with the mayonnaise. Serve garnished with walnuts and thin apple slices.   *Serves 4.*
  Suitable for slimmers if wine vinegar and lemon juice is used instead of mayonnaise.

Chicory and orange salad (illustrated opposite)

2 oranges
2 heads chicory
115 ml (4 fl. oz) French dressing
few chopped hazelnuts (optional)

660 calories
Peel and slice oranges into rings. Slice chicory thinly. Mix with dressing. Garnish with nuts. *Serves 4.*

Leeks vinaigrette

450 g (1 lb) small leeks
2 tablespoons wine vinegar
4 tablespoons corn oil
salt and pepper
1 tablespoon chopped parsley

672 calories
Clean leeks and cook in boiling salted water for 10 minutes or until just tender without being mushy. Drain well and place on serving dish. Whisk vinegar, corn oil and seasonings together with fork. Pour vinaigrette dressing over the hot leeks, sprinkle with parsley. Serve cold.   *Serves 4.*

Stuffed prunes and dates

225 g (8 oz) prunes or *dates*
few chopped nuts
few pieces stem ginger, chopped
115 g (4 oz) carton cottage cheese
1 head chicory

Suitable for slimmers   289 calories
Remove stones from prunes or dates. Mix nuts and ginger with cottage cheese. Fill stoned prunes or dates with cheese mixture. Place on bed of very finely sliced chicory. Serve as side salad.   *Serves 3.*

Fruit and cheese medley

1–2 fresh peaches
small punnet raspberries
4–6 cos lettuce leaves
225 g (8 oz) carton cottage cheese
sprig of watercress

Suitable for slimmers   285 calories
Wash peaches and cut in wedges, removing stones. Wash lettuce and raspberries, if necessary. Arrange fruit and lettuce in sections around the cottage cheese. Garnish with watercress.   *Serves 4.*

Puddings, Hot and Cold

A delicate pudding makes a perfect finish to any meal. One of the best things about the good hearted diet is that, unless you are also on a slimming campaign, you can still eat sweet things. Substituting artificial sweeteners for sugar means that slimmers can also enjoy some of the lighter recipes. The most successful puddings are those that don't try to be a pale copy of a rich egg-yolk and cream concoction; they make exciting use of the things you can eat, with the added bonus of not sitting heavily on the stomach afterwards.

Unsweetened fruit salad (illustrated on page 65)

juice of 2 sweet oranges or 115 ml (4 fl. oz)
  unsweetened orange juice
140 ml (¼ pt) cold boiled water
3–4 oranges
2–3 apples
115 g (4 oz) black grapes
115 g (4 oz) green grapes
1 peach
sprigs of mint (in season)

Suitable for slimmers   443 calories
Place juice and water in glass dish. Peel and slice oranges. Slice apples. De-seed grapes. Peel and slice peach and add all ingredients to juice. Garnish with mint sprigs. Serve very cold.   *Serves 8.*

Lemon snow (illustrated on page 64)

rind and juice of 1½ lemons
40 g (1½ oz) sugar
280 ml (½ pt) water
15 g (½ oz) gelatine
1 egg white

With sugar: 210 calories   Suitable for slimmers with sweetener: 51 calories
Peel off the yellow part of the lemon rind, avoiding the white pith. Put rind in a small pan with sugar and water. Bring to boil and strain into the gelatine. Stir until gelatine has dissolved. Allow to cool, then chill until just beginning to set. Add lemon juice and egg white. Whisk until frothy. Pile into a glass dish or individual glasses.   *Serves 4.*

Apricot amber

450 g (1 lb) apricots, without stones
2 egg whites
85 g (3 oz) sugar
or 6–7 tablets artificial sweetener

With sugar: 492 calories   Suitable for slimmers
with sweetener: 156 calories
Cook apricots, then purée. Add two-thirds sugar or
sweetener. Place in a fireproof dish. Whisk egg
whites stiffly. Add rest of sugar or sweetener. Whisk
into meringue. Place on top of apricot mixture and
bake in cool oven, 250°F, 120°C, Mark ½, for 30
minutes until meringue is lightly brown.   *Serves 4.*

   Variation: *Apple amber.* Use 450 g (1 lb) peeled
apples, cooked with a little lemon rind. Purée and
continue as for Apricot amber.

Surprise meringue

450 g (1 lb) peeled and cored cooking apples
115 g (4 oz) stoned or seedless raisins
55–115 g (2–4 oz) granulated sugar
juice of 1 or 2 oranges
1 tablespoon rum (or extra orange juice)
2 egg whites
55 g (2 oz) caster sugar

1074 calories
Slice apples and put into 1120 ml (2 pt) shallow
oven dish with raisins, granulated sugar, orange
juice and rum, if chosen. Cover with lid of foil,
cook in cool oven, 300°F, 150°C, Mark 1–2, for
40 minutes or until apples are tender, and remove
from oven. Separately whisk together whites until
stiff and gradually whisk in half caster sugar. Then
fold in remaining sugar. Pile or pipe meringue over
apples and return to oven for about 35 minutes until
meringue is set and light golden. Serve hot or
cold.   *Serves 4.*

Alison's pavlova

3 egg whites
3 tablespoons cold water
250 g (9 oz) caster sugar
1 teaspoon vinegar
1 teaspoon vanilla essence
pinch salt
3 dessertspoons cornflour
fresh or tinned peaches, strawberries or
   raspberries

Pavlova: 1190 calories   Filling: 160–300 calories
Pre-heat oven to 400°F, 200°C, Mark 5. Beat egg
whites and cold water together for 3 or 4 minutes.
Add sugar, vinegar, vanilla essence and salt, and
beat until stiff. Sprinkle on cornflour and beat for
2–3 minutes, no more. Spread in a circle, piled high
in the centre, on prepared greased paper on a cold
greased baking tray. Place in oven, turned down to
250°F, 120°C, Mark ½. Leave oven door open until
heat reaches 250°F. Cook for 1½ hours. Cool. Just
before serving, decorate with sliced fruit. *Serves 4–6.*

Lemon sherbert

1½ teaspoons unflavoured gelatine
420 ml (¾ pt) skimmed milk
170 g (6 oz) sugar
115 g (4 fl. oz) lemon juice
1 teaspoon grated lemon rind
1 egg white, stiffly beaten

884 calories
Soak gelatine in 2 tablespoons water for 5 minutes. Heat milk and sugar, add gelatine and stir until dissolved. Chill. Gradually stir in lemon juice and lemon rind. Pour into freezing tray, freeze to mush. Turn into chilled bowl and beat until fluffy, but not melted. Fold in stiffly beaten egg white. Return to freezing unit and freeze until firm.   *Serves 4.*

Slimmers' orange whip

140 ml (¼ pt) hot water
30 g (1 oz) gelatine (or enough for 560 ml (1 pt) fluid)
420 ml (¾ pt) natural orange juice
1 teaspoon lemon juice
sweetener

Suitable for slimmers   165 calories
Dissolve gelatine in hot water but do not boil. Add sweetener and lemon juice to orange juice. Add dissolved gelatine and leave to thicken slightly. Beat with a rotary whisk or in electric mixer. Place in a serving dish and put in refrigerator.   *Serves 4.*

Orange cooler

30 g (1 oz) custard powder
55 g (2 oz) sugar
560 ml (1 pt) skimmed milk
pinch salt
1 level teaspoon grated orange rind
2 oranges
4 level tablespoons redcurrant jelly
2 tablespoons water

1006 calories
Make custard sauce with first five ingredients. Pour into serving dishes and sprinkle tops with sugar to prevent a skin from forming. Leave to cool. Peel oranges, remove pith and pips and divide into segments. Arrange oranges on top of custard. Melt jelly and water together over a low heat and pour it over the oranges. Leave to cool.   *Serves 4.*

Apple mousse

450 g (1 lb) cooking apples
½ teacup water
2 tablespoons redcurrant jelly
1 egg white
ground cinnamon or *nutmeg*

319 calories
Cook apples in water. Add redcurrant jelly to hot fruit, then purée in electric blender. Whisk egg white stiffly, then add to apple when cool. Divide mixture into four glasses. Sprinkle with cinnamon or nutmeg. Chill.   *Serves 4.*

Fruit meringue

280 ml (½ pt) thick fruit purée
sugar to taste
2 egg whites

491 calories
Sweeten purée to taste. Beat egg whites until stiff. Fold half of this into purée and put in baking dish. Add 30 g (1 oz) sugar to remaining egg white and pile on top of fruit. Bake in slow oven until the meringue is set. Serve cold.   *Serves 4.*

Fruit whip

55 g (2 oz) skimmed milk powder
juice of 1 lemon
280 ml (½ pt) thick fruit purée
140 ml (¼ pt) cold water
sugar to taste
cinnamon, nutmeg, ginger, almond essence,
  or grated orange rind

545 calories
Combine milk powder and cold water and beat until smooth. Chill or refrigerate for 1 hour. Add lemon juice and beat like whipped cream. Fold in purée, sweetened to taste, and add flavourings, e.g. cinnamon, nutmeg, or ginger with apple, almond essence with apricot, or cinnamon or grated orange rind with plums or prunes. Divide into four glasses, or serve in glass bowl.   *Serves 4.*

Flummery

3 teaspoons plain flour
280 ml (½ pt) cold water
½ cup sugar
¼ cup lemon juice
3 teaspoons gelatine
3 tablespoons hot water

314 calories
Mix flour to smooth paste with a little of the cold water. Add remainder to sugar, heat to boiling, add flour gradually, and lemon rind. Cook for five minutes, stirring constantly. Add lemon juice and gelatine dissolved in hot water. Leave until thickening slightly; beat to stiff cream. Place in serving bowl. Cool. *Serves 4.*

Apple icebergs

225 g (8 oz) cooking apples
1 cup water
85 g (3 oz) sugar
1½ tablespoons semolina
560 ml (1 pt) cold custard, made with
  skimmed milk

936 calories
Peel, core and slice apples. Cook them in water with sugar. When tender, rub all through sieve. Return to pan, sprinkle in semolina while stirring, and boil, stirring, for 3 minutes. Turn into large bowl and beat for 1–2 minutes. Leave to cool. When nearly cold, beat again until white. Pour custard into glass bowl and arrange the apple mixture in rocky heaps on top. Serve as cold as possible. *Serves 4.*

Baked fruit whip

3 cups cooked prunes
4 tablespoons sugar
2 tablespoons orange juice
1 teaspoon grated orange peel
½ teaspoon cinnamon
4 egg whites

869 calories
Remove stones from prunes and mash fruit to pulp. Add 2 tablespoons sugar, orange juice, orange peel and cinnamon, blend well. Add remaining sugar to egg whites; beat until stiff. Fold prune mixture into beaten egg whites. Pile lightly into a greased 1680 ml (3 pt) casserole dish. Bake in moderate oven, 350°F, 180°C, Mark 4, for 20–30 minutes. *Serves 6.*

Lemon water ice

2 large lemons
560 ml (1 pt) water
85 g (3 oz) sugar
or 6–7 tablets artificial sweetener
1 egg white

With sugar: 282 calories   Suitable for slimmers with sweetener: 46 calories

Wash lemons and grate rinds. Squeeze juice from lemons. Put rind, sugar and water in pan, bring to boil and simmer for 10 minutes. Cool. Add lemon juice. If using sweetener, add it now. Place in freezer and freeze until mushy. Stiffly whisk egg white. Mix thoroughly into semi-frozen lemon mixture. Continue to freeze until stiff. Whisk at intervals with a fork during freezing so egg white is well mixed and the water ice freezes smoothly, otherwise the mixture is inclined to separate. *Serves 4.*

Blackcurrant, raspberry or strawberry sorbet

170 g (6 oz) sugar
or 6–7 tablets artificial sweetener
560 ml (1 pt) water
1 breakfast cup blackcurrant, raspberry or
  strawberry purée
dash of Angostura bitters (optional)
1 egg white

With sugar: 445–460 calories   Suitable for slimmers with sweetener: 110–125 calories

Make syrup by boiling together sugar and water for 5 minutes. For raspberry or strawberry, sieve fruit carefully to remove seeds. For blackcurrant, stew fruit for 5 minutes in half a cup of water, then purée, removing pips. Add Angostura to fruit mixture. Mix with syrup. For slimmers' version, add sweetener to boiled water. Mix with the fruit purée. Freeze both versions and when mushy add stiffly beaten egg white. Continue to freeze, whisking at intervals to keep mixture smooth and prevent separation. *Serves 4–6.*

Ice cream (1)

280 ml (½ pt) water
6 heaped dessertspoons skimmed milk powder
15 g (½ oz) custard powder
2–3 heaped tablespoons sugar

493 calories
Blend custard powder with half milk powder and half water. Bring slowly to boil. Allow to cool. While custard is cooling, whisk together rest of water and milk powder, adding sugar to taste. Beat two mixtures together. Freeze to mushy consistency. Beat again until mixture doubles its volume. Freeze. Yields 1 pint. *Serves 4.*

Ice cream (2)

1 level teaspoon gelatine
5 tablespoons hot water
280 ml (½ pt) cold water
5½ heaped tablespoons skimmed milk powder
2–3 heaped tablespoons sugar, according to
  taste
vanilla essence

664 calories
Dissolve gelatine in hot water. Add cold water to milk powder and sugar. Beat. Add gelatine. Beat well to mix. Freeze to mush. Beat again until mixture doubles its volume. Flavour with vanilla to taste. Freeze. Yields 1 pint. *Serves 4.*

Ice cream variations

Basic ice cream mixture number 2
225 g (8 oz) can strawberries
or 2 tablespoons stem ginger
  2 tablespoons stem ginger syrup
or 2 heaped teaspoons instant coffee
  2 tablespoons hot water
or 1 tablespoon Ribena

For strawberry variation, drain strawberries and purée before adding to basic mixture. For ginger variation, mix ginger ingredients with basic mixture. For coffee, dissolve instant coffee in water before adding to ice cream. For blackcurrant, add Ribena and whisk. If flavouring with a quantity of liquid, remember to omit the equivalent volume of cold water to keep ice cream at correct consistency.

Shortcrust pastry made with polyunsaturated margarine

85 g (3 oz) polyunsaturated margarine
2 tablespoons cold water
170 g (6 oz) plain flour
¼ teaspoon salt

1259 calories
Cream margarine and water together using a fork. Sift flour and salt together and add to margarine. Mix thoroughly and form into a firm dough. Turn on to lightly floured surface and knead gently until smooth. Roll out to 6 mm (¼ in) thickness and use as required.

Shortcrust pastry made with oil

85 ml (3 fl. oz) oil
2 tablespoons cold water
170 g (6 oz) plain flour
¼ teaspoon salt

1373 calories
Place the oil and water in a bowl. Sift together the flour and salt and gradually mix into the liquid with a fork until a manageable dough is formed. Turn on to a lightly floured board and knead gently until smooth. Roll out to 6 mm (¼ in) thickness and use as required.

Both these pastry recipes give amounts that will line one 20 cm (8 in) flan ring, or make twelve 6 cm (2½ in) tartlets, or cover one 20 cm (8 in) pie plate, or cover one 560 ml (1½ pt) pie dish.

Crumble topping
for apple, apricot, rhubarb, etc.

195 g (7 oz) plain flour
30 g (1 oz) semolina
115 g (4 oz) sugar
115 g (4 oz) polyunsaturated margarine

2226 calories
Mix all ingredients together. Spread mixture over fruit. Bake until brown at 400°F, 200°C, Mark 6.
Serves 4.

Apple and lemon soufflé

280 ml (½ pt) apple purée
grated rind of 1 lemon
2 egg whites
pinch salt
55 g (2 oz) sugar
or use artificial sweetener

With sugar: 346 calories   Suitable for slimmers with sweetener: 122 calories
Add lemon rind to apple purée. Whisk egg whites stiffly (when they are at room temperature). Add sugar or sweetener, a tablespoon at a time, whisking continuously. Using a metal spoon, fold egg white into the apple, mixing thoroughly. Pour into a straight-sided soufflé dish. Bake in pre-heated oven, 425°F, 220°C, Mark 6, for 20–25 minutes, until soufflé rises and browns slightly on top. Serve immediately.   *Serves 4.*

Apple shortcake

2 teacups plain flour
1 teaspoon baking powder
pinch salt
1 tablespoon sugar
4 tablespoons cooking oil
2 tablespoons cold water
2 large cooking apples
brown sugar
cinnamon

2194 calories
Sieve flour, baking powder and salt into a basin and add sugar. Beat oil and water together until creamy, and add to dry ingredients. Mix well, adding sufficient cold water to make a fairly stiff dough. Roll out half pastry thinly and line pie plate or 20 cm (8 in) sandwich tin. Cover with good layer of sliced apples, sprinkle with brown sugar and cinnamon, and top with layer of pastry. Seal edges, make slits in centre, and bake in fairly hot oven, about 425°F, 220°C, Mark 7, for 30–40 minutes, or until pastry is an even, golden brown. Sprinkle with icing sugar before serving. Serve hot or cold. *Serves 4–6.*

Tangy blackcurrant flan

Biscuit base:
    115 g (4 oz) digestive biscuits, crushed
    30 g (1 oz) castor sugar
    55 g (2 oz) polyunsaturated margarine

Filling:
    195 g (7 oz) can blackcurrants
    140 ml (¼ pt) blackcurrant jelly
    140 g (5 oz) carton natural yoghurt

1412 calories
Melt margarine and stir in biscuits and sugar. Press into a 20 cm (8 in) pie dish to cover sides and base. Drain blackcurrants and reserve juice. Use 85 ml (3 fl. oz) juice and heat to boiling point. Add jelly and stir until dissolved. Allow to cool slightly. Meanwhile arrange blackcurrants in flan case, reserving a few for decoration. Whisk yoghurt into cooled jelly and pour into flan case. Leave in a cool place to set for about 1½ hours. Decorate with reserved blackcurrants.   *Serves 6.*

Orange yoghurt flan

85 ml (3 fl. oz) oil
2 tablespoons cold water
170 g (6 oz) plain flour
¼ level teaspoon salt
225 g (8 oz) sugar
55 g (2 oz) cornflour
juice and grated rind of 1 orange
2 cartons low-fat natural yoghurt
2 egg whites
85 g (3 oz) caster sugar

2946 calories
Mix together oil and water with fork. Sieve together flour and salt. Gradually add to the oil and water mixture to form a rollable dough. Roll out between two sheets of greaseproof paper and use to line 20 cm (8 in) pie plate. Line with greaseproof paper and bake blind in hot oven, 400°F, 200°C, Mark 6, for 15–20 minutes. Blend together sugar, cornflour, orange juice and rind. Place in a double boiler and stir in the yoghurt. Cook over boiling water, stirring constantly, until thick and smooth. Pour into the pastry case. Whisk egg whites until stiff and dry. Add half sugar and whisk slowly until blended. Fold in remaining sugar. Pipe or pile meringue on top of flan and bake in moderately hot oven, 375°F, 190°C, Mark 5, for 5–10 minutes until lightly brown.   *Serves 4–6.*

Chiffon pie

1 tin fruit (e.g. raspberries, pineapple chunks)
fruit juice + 1 tablespoon lemon juice + water
    to 280 ml (½ pt)
2 tablespoons sugar
1 dessertspoon gelatine
2 egg whites
cold baked pie shell (18 cm (7 in) diameter)

1534 calories
Beat gelatine in a little cold fruit juice and dissolve in remainder of warmed juice and sugar. Add fruit and when nearly set fold in stiffly beaten egg whites. Pour into cold baked pie shell.   *Serves 4.*

Coffee milk jelly

30 g (1 oz) gelatine (or enough for 560 ml,
    1 pt)
1 tablespoon hot water
500 ml (18 fl. oz) skimmed milk
1 tablespoon coffee essence or strong black
    coffee
sweetener

Suitable for slimmers   211 calories
Dissolve gelatine in hot water but do not boil. Cool and stir into milk. Flavour with coffee and sweetener to taste.   *Serves 4.*
    ½ teaspoon vanilla essence may be substituted for coffee.

Chiffon tart

Shell:
    115 g (4 oz) polyunsaturated margarine
    55 g (2 oz) soft brown sugar
    85 g (3 oz) cornflakes, crushed

Filling:
    450 g (1 lb) prunes, cooked
    140 ml (¼ pt) prune juice
    100 g (3½ oz) caster sugar
    ¼ teaspoon salt
    1 tablespoon lemon juice
    rind of 1 lemon
    1 tablespoon gelatine
    40 ml (1½ fl. oz) hot water
    2 beaten egg whites, standard

2435 calories
Melt margarine and sugar together in medium-sized saucepan. Add crushed cornflakes and stir in with wooden spoon. Press mixture round base and sides of a 20 cm (8 in) pie plate. Chill well. Stone and chop prunes. Replace in saucepan and add prune juice, sugar, salt, lemon juice and rind and bring to boil. Place in liquidizer and purée, or press through sieve with wooden spoon. Dissolve gelatine in hot water, add to prune mixture. When mixture is at setting point fold in stiffly beaten egg whites. Pour into cornflake shell and allow to set. *Serves 4.*

Baked apple

1 apple, 170 g (6 oz)
sweetener to taste
mixed spice, cinnamon or nutmeg (optional)
2 tablespoons water

Suitable for slimmers   60 calories
Slice top off the apple and remove core. Sprinkle with spice and add sweetener. Replace top. Place in a heat-proof dish with 2 tablespoons water and cover with foil or lid. Bake for 30–45 minutes till soft at 350°F, 180°C, Mark 4.

Variation: stuff centre of apple with spices and orange segments. Pour over sweetener mixed with water. Bake.   (70 calories.)

Fruit juice jelly

½ packet fruit jelly
1 carton low-fat natural yoghurt
few pieces fresh fruit

400 calories
Make jelly in usual way. Chill it and before it sets, fold in 1 carton low-fat yoghurt to 280 ml (½ pt) jelly. Whisk twice before it sets. Serve garnished with fresh fruit and more yoghurt. Add soft fruit like strawberries, whole; slice oranges, apples and pears; de-seed grapes, or cut pineapple and melon into cubes.   *Serves 4.*

Low cholesterol pancakes or fritter batter

115 g (4 oz) plain flour
¼ teaspoon salt
1 egg white
280 ml (½ pt) skimmed milk
30 g (1 oz) sugar
lemon juice
cooking oil for frying

1214 calories
Sieve flour and salt into basin. Make well in centre and drop in egg white. Add half milk and beat until smooth. Gradually add remaining milk, beating all the time until thin batter is obtained. Cook in hot oiled pan in usual manner. Sprinkle with sugar and lemon juice.   *Serves 4.*

Alternatively serve with maple syrup or with the following sauce.

Orange pancake sauce

juice and grated rind of 1 small orange
juice of 1 small lemon
2 dessertspoons arrowroot
1 tablespoon golden syrup
1 orange, chopped segments and grated rind

293 calories
Make orange and lemon juice up to 280 ml (½ pt) with water. Mix arrowroot to smooth paste with a little fruit juice and water. Heat remaining juice, add syrup, stir until dissolved, then pour over arrowroot. Return to pan and cook, stirring well until sauce thickens. Add chopped orange segments and grated rind. Roll up pancakes and pour sauce over.   *Serves 4.*

Apple fritters

450 g (1 lb) cooking apples
55 g (2 oz) flour
pinch salt
1 level dessertspoon caster sugar
1 tablespoon oil
40 ml (⅛ pt) tepid water
1 egg white
a little cooking oil for frying

1087 calories
Peel, core and slice apples. Sieve flour, salt and sugar into basin. Make well in centre and add oil and water. Stir to form smooth batter. Fold in stiffly beaten egg white. Heat oil to 375°F, 190°C. Coat apple rings in batter and fry in heated oil for approximately 3–4 minutes. Drain well on kitchen paper. Sprinkle with caster sugar before serving.   *Serves 4.*

Baked bananas with lemon sauce

15 g (½ oz) polyunsaturated margarine
55 g (2 oz) soft brown sugar
pinch ground nutmeg or cinnamon
grated rind and juice of 1 lemon
2 level teaspoons cornflour
3 tablespoons water
4 small bananas

437 calories
Place margarine, sugar, nutmeg, lemon juice and rind into saucepan. Blend cornflour with water and stir into pan. Bring to boil, stirring all the time. Peel bananas and add to pan, whole or cut into pieces as liked. Cover pan and cook gently for 10 minutes. Serve hot or cold.   *Serves 4.*

Baked apricot soufflé

20 g (¾ oz) polyunsaturated margarine
20 g (¾ oz) flour
225 g (8 oz) fresh stewed apricots
  to provide 70 g (2½ oz) purée and 140 ml
  (¼ pt) juice or use tinned apricots
30 g (1 oz) sugar
3 egg whites

Sauce:
  140 ml (¼ pt) apricot juice
  1 level teaspoon arrowroot
  sugar and colouring

494 calories
Make panada with margarine, flour, apricot purée and juice and cook till thick. Cool. Add sugar and fold in stiffly beaten egg whites. Pour mixture into prepared soufflé dish and bake in a moderate oven, 350°F, 180°C, Mark 4, until well risen and firm, about 45 minutes to 1 hour. To make sauce: thicken apricot juice with arrowroot; add sugar and colouring. Serve in a sauce boat.   *Serves 3–4.*

Rhubarb and ginger pie

(illustrated opposite)

675 g (1½ lb) rhubarb
30 g (1 oz) crystallized or stem ginger, chopped
15 g (½ oz) sugar
170 g (6 oz) shortcrust pastry
a little skimmed milk or beaten egg white for glazing

1090 calories

Prepare rhubarb and cut into 25 mm (1 in) lengths. Layer fruit, ginger and sugar in a 20 cm (8 in) pie dish. Roll out pastry to measure at least 25 mm (1 in) larger than the pie dish. Lay 12 mm (½ in) strips around wetted rim of dish. Brush with water. Lay large piece of pastry on top of fruit. Press edges gently together. Trim off surplus, knock up and flute the edges. Make a hole in the centre for steam to escape. Brush with milk or beaten egg white. Bake at 375°F, 190°C, Mark 5, for 40–50 minutes, until golden brown.   *Serves 4.*

Summer pudding

(illustrated opposite)

225 g (8 oz) fresh or frozen fruit
30–55 g (1–2 oz) sugar
140 ml (¼ pt) water
115–170 g (4–6 oz) stale bread or cake (4–6 slices of a large loaf)

668 calories

The best fruits to use are raspberries, loganberries, blackcurrants, red plums. Stew fruit with sugar and water until tender. Cut bread or cake into 6 cm (¼ in) thick slices. Cut fingers or triangles to line a 560 ml (1 pt) basin, reserving enough whole slices for lid. Half fill lined basin with fruit, add a layer of bread or cake, then rest of fruit, and finally a lid of bread or cake. Pour over juice; cover with weighted plate to fit inside basin. Chill for several hours. Unmould and garnish with fruit. Serve with skimmed-milk custard.   *Serves 4.*

Apple flan

(illustrated opposite)

170 g (6 oz) shortcrust pastry
3 tablespoons apricot jam
675 g (1½ lb) cooking apples
grated rind of ½ lemon
30 g (1 oz) polyunsaturated margarine
15 g (½ oz) sugar
1–2 red-skinned eating apples
1 teaspoon water

1636 calories

Line 20 cm (8 in) flan ring with pastry. Spread 1 tablespoon of jam over base. Peel, core and slice cooking apples and cook gently until soft. Purée apples, then stir in lemon rind, margarine and sugar. Spoon into pastry case. Arrange sliced eating apple on top. Bake in a fairly hot oven, 375°F, 190°C, Mark 5, for 20 minutes, then reduce heat to 325°F, 160°C, Mark 3, for further 20 minutes. Sieve remaining jam, add water and bring to boil stirring continuously. Spoon over top of flan. Note: If the purée seems too wet thicken with a little cornflour or arrowroot.   *Serves 4.*

Snacks and Savouries

This selection of easy recipes fills a problematical gap. Dishes using cheese and whole eggs are favourite stand-bys for snack meals, and when these two ingredients need to be restricted, finding something quick to take their place can be difficult. The recipes in this section can be used for light lunches or suppers and bolstered into main meal dishes with the accompaniment of vegetables or a salad. Some, like the savoury flans, can also be used as starters for a party meal.

Smoked haddock flan (illustrated opposite)

170 g (6 oz) shortcrust pastry (page 86)
225 g (8 oz) smoked haddock, poached in a
  little milk until tender
1 small tin sweetcorn, drained
30 g (1 oz) flour
30 g (1 oz) polyunsaturated margarine
280 ml (½ pt) skimmed milk
salt and pepper

1739 calories
Use pastry to line a 20 cm (8 in) flan ring. Bake blind at 375°F, 190°C, Mark 5, for 30 minutes. Drain haddock, flake with fork and mix with sweetcorn. Melt margarine in saucepan, stir in flour and cook for 1 minute. Gradually blend in skimmed milk to make thick white sauce. Remove pan from the heat. Combine sauce with haddock, season to taste and pour mixture into flan case. Garnish with tomato slices or lemon twists and serve. *Serves 4.*

Ratatouille flan (illustrated opposite)

170 g (6 oz) shortcrust pastry (page 86)
4 small courgettes, sliced
1 small aubergine, chopped or sliced
1 small green pepper, seeded and chopped
2 small onions, skinned and sliced
1 clove garlic (optional)
1 small tin tomato purée
2 tablespoons oil
salt and pepper

1157 calories
Use pastry to line a 20 cm (8 in) flan ring. Bake blind at 375°F, 190°C, Mark 5, for 25–30 minutes until golden brown. Meanwhile, place remaining ingredients in a large, strong saucepan, cover with lid and simmer gently for about 1 hour or until vegetables are soft. Pile the vegetable mixture into the flan case and serve hot or cold. *Serves 4.*

Bacon flan (illustrated on page 94)

170 g (6 oz) shortcrust pastry (page 86)
2 rashers lean bacon, with rind and fat removed
15 g (½ oz) polyunsaturated margarine
1 small onion, chopped
1 small tin mushrooms, drained
1 chicken stock cube
170 ml (6 fl. oz) hot water
2½ tablespoons skimmed milk powder
2 egg whites
¼ teaspoon oregano
salt and pepper
1 tomato, sliced

Use pastry to line a 20 cm (8 in) flan ring. Bake blind at 375°F, 190°C, Mark 5, for 10 minutes. Grill bacon and chop into small pieces. Heat margarine and gently fry onion until tender. Mix together the bacon, onion and mushrooms and place in flan case. Dissolve stock cube in hot water. Whisk in dried milk and egg whites until thoroughly blended. Add oregano and season with salt and pepper. Pour this mixture into flan case and top with slices of tomato. Bake the flan at 375°F, 190°C, Mark 5, for 20–25 minutes or until golden brown and set. Serve hot or cold.   *Serves 4.*

Cheese, oatmeal and tomato pie

Pastry to line 18 cm (7 in) diameter, 25 mm (1 in) deep flan dish
30 g (1 oz) polyunsaturated margarine
30 g (1 oz) oatmeal
280 ml (½ pt) bottled tomato pulp or 6 tinned peeled tomatoes
1 tablespoon tomato juice
salt, pepper, mustard, parsley
6 portions vegetarian cheese, grated

3657 calories
Line flan dish thinly with pastry. Melt margarine in saucepan, blend in oatmeal, stirring well with wooden spoon. Gradually add tomato until mixture is soft and creamy. Cook well, stirring all the time, add seasonings and grated cheese. Put mixture in pastry case, bake in moderately hot oven, 375°F, 190°C, Mark 5, for 20–30 minutes until golden brown. Serve at once, garnished with parsley.
Serves 3.

Cornish pasties

225 g (8 oz) flour
115 g (4 oz) polyunsaturated margarine
1 teaspoon baking powder
cold water

Filling:
115 g (4 oz) finely chopped meat
115 g (4 oz) raw potato, grated
55 g (2 oz) onion, finely chopped
salt, pepper, pinch off a beef stock cube

2018 calories
Rub fat into flour and baking powder. Mix with cold water to a stiff dough. Roll out dough and cut 4 circles 15 cm (6 in) in diameter. Mix filling ingredients and divide between pastry circles. Moisten edges with water and fold over in half. Crimp edges securely together. Bake for 15 minutes at 400°F, 200°C, Mark 6, then reduce heat to 325°F, 160°C, Mark 3, and continue cooking for another 45 minutes.   *Serves 4.*

Pizza (illustrated on page 65)

Dough:
  225 g (8 oz) flour
  1 level teaspoon salt
  15 g (½ oz) polyunsaturated margarine
  15 g (½ oz) fresh yeast
  or 7 g (¼ oz) dried yeast
  1 small teaspoon sugar
  115–140 ml (4–5 fl. oz) tepid water

225 g (8 oz) tinned tomatoes
55 g (2 oz) mushrooms
115 g (4 oz) chicken or ham
115 g (4 oz) cottage cheese
salt, pepper, paprika, mixed herbs

1360 calories
Sift flour and salt into a warm basin. Rub margarine into flour. Cream yeast and sugar, mix with tepid water. Add to flour and beat thoroughly. Leave to rise for 20–30 minutes in a warm place till double in size. Divide the dough into two 20 cm (8 in) rounds; brush with oil. Chop mushrooms and fry in minimum oil. Drain tomatoes. Finely chop chicken or ham. Mix cottage cheese, tomatoes, mushrooms, meat and seasonings together. Spread on rounds of dough and bake in a hot oven, 425°F, 220°C, Mark 7, till dough is risen and cooked, about 20 minutes. *Serves 4.*

Lentil rissoles

55 g (2 oz) lentils
7 g (¼ oz) polyunsaturated margarine
1 small onion, finely chopped
195 ml (7 fl. oz) water
salt, pepper
1 teaspoon ketchup
1 tablespoon semolina
breadcrumbs for coating

Suitable for slimmers   400 calories
Wash lentils. Melt margarine and fry onion for a few minutes. Add lentils and toss. Add water, seasoning and ketchup. Simmer for about 1 hour till soft. Sprinkle in the semolina and cook for 5 minutes, stirring well. Turn on to plate and cool. Shape into rolls or patties. Coat with breadcrumbs and fry till brown. *Serves 2.*

  This is a useful recipe for vegetarians. It is also inexpensive and much more delicious than it actually sounds.

Suppertime kedgeree

115 g (4 oz) rice
½ tablespoon cooking oil
1 hard-boiled egg white, chopped
170 g (6 oz) cooked haddock
seasoning, ½ teaspoon curry powder
fresh chopped parsley or chives
½ cup cooked peas or sweetcorn kernels

Suitable for slimmers   771 calories
Cook rice. Flake fish. Place oil in pan. Add curry powder, egg white, rice, flaked fish, and peas or sweetcorn. Heat thoroughly. Mix in herbs, reserving some for garnish.   *Serves 2.*

Paella

3 tablespoons corn oil
1 onion, finely chopped
115 g (4 oz) raw chicken, diced
170 g (6 oz) long grain rice
1 mixed herb stock cube, dissolved in 420 ml
   (¾ pt) water
½ level teaspoon turmeric
55 g (2 oz) frozen peas
220 g (7¾ oz) tin tuna fish, flaked
1 red pepper, sliced

1555 calories
Heat oil and fry onion and chicken for 5 minutes. Add rice and cook for further minute. Pour in mixed herb stock, and turmeric, peas, tuna and pepper. Bring to boil, cover tightly and simmer for 15 minutes until all liquid is absorbed.   *Serves 4.*

Snack patties

225 g (8 oz) cooked meat
30 g (1 oz) polyunsaturated margarine
1 onion, finely chopped
225 g (8 oz) cold mashed potatoes
seasoning
½ teaspoon grated lemon rind
1 teaspoon chopped parsley
pinch nutmeg
skimmed milk and flour for coating
cooking oil

1172 calories
Chop meat finely. Melt margarine and fry onion gently to soften. Mix with meat and potato. Add seasoning, lemon rind, parsley and nutmeg. Form into small flat cakes. Dip in milk and flour. Fry in oil until golden brown. Drain on kitchen paper to blot excess fat. Serve immediately with grilled tomatoes.   *Serves 4.*

Chicken crispies

140 ml (¼ pt) savoury white sauce:
  30 g (1 oz) flour
  30 g (1 oz) polyunsaturated margarine
  140 ml (¼ pt) stock, using cube or
    skimmed milk
225 g (8 oz) chopped cooked chicken
seasoning
rolled oats for coating
cooking oil for frying

1180 calories
Make up sauce from flour, margarine and stock or milk. Stir in chicken and divide into four. Shape each portion into a pyramid. Coat in rolled oats. Heat oil to 375°F, 19°C, in deep pan. Fry chicken for 2-3 minutes until golden brown. Serve hot or cold. *Serves 4.*

Mediterranean meat balls

565 g (1¼ lb) lean minced beef
1 teaspoon lemon juice
grated rind of 1 medium lemon
55 g (2 oz) fine dry breadcrumbs
1 egg white
1 medium onion, finely chopped
1 teaspoon salt, freshly ground pepper
½ teaspoon mixed herbs
1 cup beef stock
small tin tomato paste
2 teaspoons cornflour
2 tablespoons cold water

1300 calories
Mix meat, lemon rind and juice, breadcrumbs, egg white, onion and seasonings. Add half stock. Mix again and leave to stand for 15 minutes. Form into six meat balls. Place on baking dish and bake at 350°F, 180°C, Mark 4, for 30 minutes. Make sauce by mixing remaining stock with tomato paste. Add seasoning. Mix cornflour with cold water. Add to sauce. Bring to boil, stirring until smooth. Simmer for 5 minutes. Add to meat balls. Bake for further 15 minutes. *Serves 6.*

Fish fingers

335 g (12 oz) thick haddock, cod or whiting
  fillets
cooking oil for frying
Batter:
  2 dessertspoons flour
  2 tablespoons skimmed milk
  pinch salt
or seasoned flour
skimmed milk
dried breadcrumbs

Fried: 624 calories Suitable for slimmers if baked: 360 calories
Cut fish into 75 × 25 mm (3 × 1 in) strips like fish fingers. If using batter, mix flour and skimmed milk together with salt. Dip fish into this and shallow fry in hot oil. *Or* dip fish in seasoned flour, milk and then breadcrumbs, and fry or bake in the oven at 350°F, 180°C, Mark 4, for 20 minutes. *Serves 4.*

Spaghetti Milanese

170 g (6 oz) spaghetti
3 tablespoons cooking oil
1 onion, chopped
1 clove garlic, crushed
420 g (15 oz) tin peeled tomatoes
2 tablespoons tomato purée
2 mixed herb stock cubes
115 g (4 oz) cooked ham, diced
55 g (2 oz) mushrooms, sliced

1370 calories
Cook spaghetti in boiling salted water until tender. Heat oil and sauté onion and garlic for 2–3 minutes. Add tomatoes, tomato purée and mixed herb cubes, bring to boil stirring. Add cooked ham and mushrooms, cover and simmer for 10 minutes. Serves 4.

Fast spaghetti

225 g (8 oz) spaghetti
1 onion, peeled and chopped
1 clove garlic
1 tablespoon cooking oil
675 g (1½ lb) tin tomatoes
1 glass wine (optional)
1 tin condensed consommé
4 tablespoons chopped cooked meat, if available
1 tin sweetcorn, drained
1 bay leaf
mixed herbs and seasoning
few chopped olives

Without meat: 1270 calories. With meat: 1510 calories
Cook spaghetti in plenty of boiling water. Meanwhile fry onion and garlic gently in oil for 5 minutes. Add all the other ingredients, bring to boil and simmer until spaghetti is cooked. Drain and place on serving dish. Add the sauce. Garnish with chopped fresh herbs and a few chopped olives. Serves 4.

Chicken croquettes

1 cup minced chicken or turkey
½ cup thick white sauce:
    30 g (1 oz) polyunsaturated margarine
    30 g (1 oz) flour
    140 ml (¼ pt) skimmed milk
½ teaspoon chopped parsley
1 tablespoon finely sliced mushrooms, sautéed in polyunsaturated margarine
1 teaspoon lemon juice (fresh or bottled)
1 dessertspoon sherry (optional)

670 calories
Mix all ingredients together. Form into rounds or sausage shapes. Roll in seasoned flour and dip in breadcrumbs, then in skimmed milk and again in breadcrumbs. Fry until golden brown in hot oil. Drain on absorbent paper.   Serves 4.

Baked potato snack

1 large potato
1–2 tablespoons skimmed milk
½ teaspoon polyunsaturated margarine
pinch pepper
¼ level teaspoon salt
1 tablespoon chopped parsley or *finely chopped
  cooked meats*
½ tablespoon chopped fried onion

248 calories
Scrub potato and brush skin with oil, or rub with greased paper. Place on baking shelf and cook until it feels soft when squeezed with a cloth. Cut in half lengthwise and scoop out the inside carefully. Mash this with milk, fat, seasonings and other chosen ingredients. Put back in the shell, brown in a hot oven for a few minutes, 400–425°F, 200–220° C, Mark 6–7.

Variations: 1. Fill with minced lean meat or flaked white fish. Moisten with a little fatless sauce and add chopped parsley. 2. Mix potato with a little vegetable extract and moisten with skimmed milk. 3. Mix with skimmed milk, cottage cheese, and chopped green herbs.

Sardines on toast

130 g (4½ oz) tin sardines in oil
lemon juice
2 slices of toast

Suitable for slimmers   353 calories
Drain sardines by putting in a wire sieve. Pour boiling water over them to remove excess oil. Mash into a soft paste with lemon juice. Spread on toast and place under the grill to cook for a few moments.   *Serves 2.*

Sardine savouries

Shortcrust pastry:
  115 g (4 oz) flour
  55 g (2 oz) polyunsaturated margarine
  ½ teaspoon baking powder
130 g (4½ oz) tin sardines in oil
lemon juice

1239 calories
Make pastry and roll out into a long strip. Drain sardines by putting in a wire sieve. Pour boiling water over them to remove excess oil. Mash with lemon juice. Spread on pastry strip and roll up like a Swiss roll. Cut into circles and bake in a hot oven, 400°F, 200°C, Mark 6, for 10–15 minutes till lightly brown. A good party snack.

Stuffed tomatoes (1)

4 large tomatoes
30–55 g (1–2 oz) fresh breadcrumbs
1 small onion, finely chopped
1 tablespoon chopped parsley, oregano or
    chervil
30 g (1 oz) polyunsaturated margarine,
    melted
salt, pepper

320 calories
Cut tops off tomatoes and reserve lids. Scoop centres into a basin. Add crumbs, onion, herbs, margarine and seasoning and mix well. Pile back into tomato cases and put lids back on. Place in greased dish and heat in a fairly hot oven at 400°F, 200°C, Mark 6, for 15 minutes.   *Serves 2.*

Variations: 1. Use 55 g (2 oz) chopped lobster instead of onion. 2. Use 55 g (2 oz) cooked lean lamb, finely chopped.

Stuffed tomatoes (2)

6 medium-sized firm tomatoes

Filling:
    15 g ($\frac{1}{2}$ oz) polyunsaturated margarine
    1 teaspoon chopped onion
    2–3 fresh mushrooms, chopped
    55 g (2 oz) chopped cooked chicken
    2 tablespoons white breadcrumbs
    a little sauce or tomato pulp
    pinch ground mace, cayenne, salt
dried breadcrumbs

Suitable for slimmers   368 calories
Wipe the tomatoes and cut a small round from each at the end opposite the stalk. Scoop out all the pulp from the inside and turn cases upside down for a short time to drain. Melt polyunsaturated margarine in a pan and fry onion and mushrooms until cooked. Add chicken and other ingredients, making the mixture rather soft. Fill tomatoes with this, sprinkle with breadcrumbs and bake in a moderate oven, 350°F, 180°C, Mark 4, for 12–15 minutes.   *Serves 3.*

Ledsham tomatoes

4 large tomatoes
1 teaspoon dry mustard
55 g (2 oz) lean cooked ham
55 g (2 oz) cottage cheese
seasoning, paprika
chopped chives
little brown sugar (optional)

Suitable for slimmers.   237 calories
Slice tops from tomatoes. Scoop out insides into bowl, separating juice from flesh. Mix 1 teaspoon dry mustard with tomato juice. Chop ham; add to tomato flesh and mustard. Add cheese. Mix and season to taste. Add chopped chives and fill tomatoes liberally. Place in baking dish. Add pinch brown sugar to top of each tomato. Bake at 350°F, 180°C, Mark 4, for 15–20 minutes till tops are brown. Serve hot.   *Serves 2.*

Spinach soufflé

140 ml (¼ pt) spinach purée
20 g (¾ oz) polyunsaturated margarine
20 g (¾ oz) flour
salt, pepper
1½ tablespoons skimmed milk powder
2 egg whites

Suitable for slimmers   440 calories
Make Panada style sauce with spinach purée, flour and margarine. Add seasonings and skimmed milk powder. Cool slightly. Fold in stiffly beaten egg whites. Turn into a greased fireproof dish and bake in a moderately hot oven, 350°F, 180°C, Mark 4, for 30–40 minutes, till well risen and firm to touch. Serve immediately.   *Serves 2–3.*

Savoury soufflé

20 g (¾ oz) flour
20 g (¾ oz) polyunsaturated margarine
140 ml (¼ pt) skimmed milk
85 g (3 oz) minced cooked meat, e.g. ham or chicken
salt, pepper
2 egg whites

Suitable for slimmers   490 calories
Make Panada style sauce with fat, flour, and skimmed milk. Stir in minced meat and add seasoning. Fold in stiffly beaten egg whites and turn into a greased fireproof dish. Bake in a moderately hot oven, 350°F, 180°C, Mark 4, for 30 minutes, till well risen and firm to the touch. Serve immediately.
Serves 2–3.

Quick risotto

1 cup raw rice
thyme
bay leaf
clove
1 onion, diced
2 tablespoons cooking oil
335 g (12 oz) pre-cooked diced lean meat

About 1148 calories
Cook rice in boiling water with thyme, bay leaf and clove. Fry onion in oil, add rice and brown slightly. Add meat and heat through. Serve with peas or green beans.   *Serves 4.*

Cottager's ham

2 tablespoons cooking oil
115 g (4 oz) onions, chopped
1 large packet frozen peas
140 ml (¼ pt) water
salt and pepper
55 g (2 oz) lean ham, chopped

Suitable for slimmers   517 calories
Heat oil and fry onions without browning for 5 minutes. Add peas, water, salt and pepper, simmer for 5 minutes. Add ham, cover and simmer for 10 minutes. (55 g (2 oz) ham is sufficient only to flavour peas. More may be added if required.) *Serves 4.*

Tripe and onions

450 g (1 lb) prepared tripe
560 ml (1 pt) skimmed milk (hot)
225 g (8 oz) onions
salt and pepper
30 g (1 oz) polyunsaturated margarine
30 g (1 oz) flour

1050 calories
Cut tripe into strips about 75 × 38 mm (3 × 1½ in). Place in a casserole with sliced onions, salt, pepper and hot skimmed milk. Cook for 1 hour in a moderate oven, 325°F, 160°C, Mark 3. When cooked, make a sauce by melting margarine in a pan, adding flour and cooking very slowly till it forms a roux but does not brown. Gradually add the milk stock from the tripe and bring to boil, stirring all the time. Simmer for 3–5 minutes. Pour over tripe and serve with toast.   *Serves 4.*

Use only occasionally.

Slimmers' rarebit

15 g (½ oz) polyunsaturated margarine
15 g (½ oz) flour
3 tablespoons skimmed milk
salt and pepper
115 g (4 oz) cottage cheese
1 teaspoon made mustard
dash Worcestershire sauce
pinch cayenne
1 tablespoon beer if available

Suitable for slimmers   293 calories
Melt margarine, add flour and then milk. Cook throughly. Beat in the seasoning, cheese, mustard, Worcestershire sauce, cayenne and beer. Pour over hot toast.   *Serves 2.*

Cottage cheese and ham rarebit

4 thick slices bread
225 g (8 oz) cottage cheese
55 g (2 oz) lean chopped ham
salt, pepper
1 teaspoon made mustard

1219 calories
Cut crusts from bread and toast on one side. On untoasted side spread mixture of cottage cheese, ham and seasonings. Place under hot grill and cook until cheese begins to bubble. Serve immediately. *Serves 2–4.*

Toast toppers

1 slice white or brown bread

Mushroom topping (per person):
   2 small mushrooms, finely chopped
   1 small tomato, finely chopped
   1 tablespoon sweet pickle

Fish topping (per person):
   2 tablespoons tuna fish, drained and flaked
   1 teaspoon lemon juice

Suitable for slimmers With mushrooms: 136 calories   With fish: 210 calories
Toast one side of bread. Mix topping well together and spread evenly on untoasted side of bread. Replace under grill for a few minutes to brown.

Sandwich fillings with cooked meats

Beef:
  + *mustard*
  + *pickle*
  + *chopped spring onion*
  + *tomato*
Chicken:
  + *cress*
  + *cottage cheese*
  + *salad vegetables*
  + *gherkins*
Ham:
  + *gherkins*
  + *tomato ketchup*
  + *cottage cheese and chives*
Pork:
  + *grated apple and lemon juice*
  + *mango chutney*

These can be prepared in advance, foil-wrapped and stored in a home freezer to save time when meals are taken to work or school and picnics prepared. If taken out before work a package will be thawed in time for lunch.

Toasted sandwiches

Chopped cooked chicken and special
  mayonnaise (page 68)
Marmite and tomato slices
Chopped ham and French mustard
Crispy bacon and ketchup
Eggless lemon spread
Mushrooms, fried in oil
Cooking oil, brown sugar and cinnamon

Grill bread on one side. Spread filling on untoasted side, then heat under grill. Serve very hot.

Cottage cheese fillings

Chopped chives *Parsley*
Spring onion *Mint*
Gherkin *Sliced radishes*
Watercress *Pineapple*
Celery *Marmite*
Tomato *Lettuce*
Cucumber *Walnuts*

Combine cottage cheese with any of these fillings for variety of flavour.

Sandwich fillings with fish

Sardines (drained of olive oil)   *Salmon*
Smoked cod or haddock   *Tuna*
White flaked fish   *Pilchards*
Kipper   *Herring*
Anchovies

Combine with a savoury sauce or vinegar to make moist and easy to spread.

Sandwich fillings with vegetables

Celery   *Mustard and cress*
Chives   *Radishes*
Watercress   *Grated carrot*
Spring onion   *Fried mushrooms*
Cucumber   *Gherkins*
Lettuce   *Crushed sweetcorn*
Tomato   *(tinned)*
Beetroot   *Parsley*
Chicory   *Mint*
Onion   *French runner beans*

Calorie value depends upon filling chosen.

Vegetables may be chopped and combined using special low-cholesterol mayonnaise or other low animal fat sauces to bind them. Chopped fruits, nuts, cottage cheese, hard-boiled egg white and Marmite also mix well with some vegetables.

Sandwich fillings with fruit

Banana, mashed
  + lemon juice and brown sugar
Apple, grated
  + celery, beetroot and mayonnaise
  + celery, walnuts and mayonnaise
  + dates or raisins
Dates, mashed
  + lemon or orange juice
  + lemon juice and apple
  + lemon juice and nuts
Raisins, chopped
  + honey and lemon juice
  + grated apple
Pineapple, crushed
  + cottage cheese

Use the polyunsaturated margarine to spread on bread, preferably brown bread, which enhances the flavour of the fruit.

Hot bread

Vienna loaf + one of the flavoured
* 'butters' below*

Slice the loaf in half lengthways. Spread the flavoured margarine generously along the cut sides and sandwich the bread back together. Wrap the bread in foil and place in a hot oven, 400°F, 200°C, Mark 7, for approximately 7 minutes. Serve the hot bread with soups, stews and casseroles.

Garlic 'butter'

2 cloves garlic
55 g (2 oz) polyunsaturated margarine

445 calories
Peel the garlic cloves and blanch in boiling water for 3 minutes. Drain and chop very finely. Cream the margarine and beat in garlic.

Mixed herb 'butter'

55 g (2 oz) polyunsaturated margarine
1 teaspoon dried mixed herbs
1 teaspoon lemon juice

445 calories
Cream the margarine and beat in the herbs and lemon juice.

Paprika 'butter'

55 g (2 oz) polyunsaturated margarine
1 teaspoon paprika
pinch salt

445 calories
Cream the margarine and beat in the paprika and salt.

Baking

This diet does mean that bought cakes are on the banned list because you can't be sure they contain the right ingredients. The baking recipes are designed to lure you away from the cake shop and into the kitchen to whip up your own selection of crisp tea breads and delicious cakes or biscuits. Home baking makes more economic sense than buying cakes. Also there is nothing quite as special as the flavour of home-made cakes. These recipes concentrate on biscuits and cakes that do not need the addition of butter and egg yolks. It is worth remembering though, that polyunsaturated margarine can always be substituted for butter for home-baked cakes.

Bran loaf

225 g (8 oz) wholemeal flour
225 g (8 oz) strong flour
115 g (4 oz) bran
2 teaspoons salt
1 tablespoon oil
Yeast liquid:
   30 g (1 oz) fresh yeast
   335 ml (12 fl. oz) warm water
or
   1 teaspoon sugar
   335 ml (12 fl. oz) warm water
   3 teaspoons dried yeast

2040 calories
Place flours, bran and salt in bowl. Add oil and frothy yeast liquid; mix to firm dough. Turn on to a lightly floured surface and knead well for 5 minutes. Place in oiled polythene bag and leave to prove in a warm place for about 1 to 1½ hours. Turn risen dough out on to floured surface and flatten with knuckles. Divide into two. Shape to fit two oiled 450 g (1 lb) loaf tins. Brush tops with salt water and place in oiled polythene bags. Leave in warm place until double in size. Bake at 450°F, 230°C, Mark 8, for about 45 minutes or until the loaves sound hollow when tapped.

White plait (Illustrated on page 111)

675 g (1½ lb) strong flour
2 teaspoons salt
1 teaspoon sugar
15 g (½ oz) polyunsaturated margarine

Yeast liquid:
   30 g (1 oz) fresh yeast
   420 ml (15 fl. oz) warm water
   25 mg tablet ascorbic acid

2515 calories
Blend yeast in water with crushed tablet of ascorbic acid. Rub margarine into flour, salt and sugar. Pour in yeast liquid and form into firm dough. Turn on to lightly floured surface; knead for 10 minutes. Divide in half. For each half: cut into 3 pieces, roll pieces into strands, plait together and pinch ends. Brush with skimmed milk and sprinkle with poppy seeds. Place on oiled tray and cover with polythene bag. Leave to rise in warm place until double in size. Bake in hot oven, 450°F, 230°C, Mark 8, for about 30–35 minutes.

French onion bread (Illustrated opposite)

450 g (1 lb) strong flour
½ teaspoon salt
1 tablespoon sugar
1 tablespoon oil
40 g (1½ oz) French onion soup mix
225 ml (fl. oz) water
Yeast liquid:
    15 g (½ oz) fresh yeast
    115 ml (4 fl. oz) warm water
or 1 teaspoon sugar
    115 ml (4 fl. oz) warm water
    2 teaspoons dried yeast

1927 calories
Place flour, salt and sugar in bowl. Combine oil, soup mix and water; bring to boil and simmer for 10 minutes. Cool and add to flour with yeast liquid. Mix to firm dough, turn on to floured surface and knead until smooth. Place in oiled polythene bag and leave in warm place to rise until double, about 1 hour. Turn dough on to floured surface and flatten with knuckles. Divide into two. Shape pieces into ovals. Place on floured baking sheet. With sharp knife make diagonal cuts on top, about 3 mm (⅛ in) deep and 25 mm (1 in) apart. Brush with a little beaten egg white, cover with polythene. Leave to prove until almost double in size, about 30 minutes. Bake at 375°F, 190°C, Mark 5, about 25 minutes or until crisp and brown. *Makes 2 small batons.*

Wholemeal rolls (Illustrated opposite)

450 g (1 lb) wholemeal flour
1 teaspoon salt
1 teaspoon sugar
1 tablespoon oil

Yeast liquid:
    30 g (1 oz) fresh yeast
    280 ml (½ pt) warm water
or
    1 teaspoon sugar
    280 ml (½ pt) warm water
    1 tablespoon dried yeast

1658 calories
Blend fresh yeast in warm water *or* dissolve sugar in warm water and sprinkle on dried yeast. Leave until frothy – about 10 minutes. Mix together flour, salt, sugar, oil and yeast liquid to form a dough. Turn on to floured surface and knead until smooth and no longer sticky, about 4 minutes. Place dough in oiled polythene bag and leave in warm place until double in size, about 1 hour. Turn dough on to floured surface and flatten with knuckles. Divide dough into 55 g (2 oz) pieces and form into small balls. Place on floured baking sheets. Cut a cross on top for decoration. Cover with polythene and leave to prove in warm place until almost double in size, about 20–30 minutes. Bake at 450°F, 230°C, Mark 8, for about 20 minutes or until golden brown and crisp. *Makes 12 rolls.*

Tea loaf (Illustrated opposite)

280 g (10 oz) plain flour
1 rounded teaspoon bicarbonate of soda
½ rounded teaspoon cream of tartar
pinch salt
85 g (3 oz) sugar
115 g (4 oz) polyunsaturated margarine
115 g (4 oz) sultanas
55 g (2 oz) chopped walnuts
skimmed milk to mix

2968 calories

Mix dry ingredients, rub in margarine and add fruit and nuts. Add milk until mixture is of 'dropping' consistency. Bake in greased and lined loaf tin for about 1 hour in a moderate oven, 350°F, 180°C, Mark 4, until loaf is light brown and springy to touch and beginning to leave sides of tin. Sultanas and walnuts can be substituted with:

115 g (4 oz) chopped dates, 115 g (4 oz) sultanas, using only 55 g (2 oz) sugar *or* 115 g (4 oz) each of sultanas and currants with a little mixed peel *or* 225 g (8 oz) dates *or* 225 g (8 oz) preserved ginger.

Fruit cake (Illustrated opposite)

115 g (4 oz) polyunsaturated margarine
225 g (8 oz) sugar
450 g (1 lb) plain flour
15 g (½ oz) bicarbonate of soda
pinch salt
115 g (4 oz) currants
225 g (8 oz) mixed raisins and sultanas
30 g (1 oz) peel
4 tablespoons skimmed milk
½ wineglass vinegar

4667 calories

Melt margarine and sugar together. Mix into flour very slowly. Stir in other ingredients slowly. Add vinegar last. Put in prepared tin, place in a moderate oven, 350°F, 180°C, Mark 4, and bake for 1½ hours. Use a large square or oblong cake tin. This cake should last one person about 10–14 days.

Orange feather cake (Illustrated opposite)

115 g (4 oz) polyunsaturated margarine
115 g (4 oz) caster sugar
rind of 1 orange
5 egg whites, stiffly beaten
115 g (4 oz) plain flour, sifted with
    1 teaspoon baking powder

Orange icing:
    85 g (3 oz) polyunsaturated margarine
    225 g (8 oz) sieved icing sugar
    2 dessertspoons orange juice

3486 calories

Cream margarine and sugar together until light and fluffy. Stir in orange rind. Fold in egg whites and flour alternately. Place in greased and floured 18 cm (7 in) cake tin. Bake at 350°F, 180°C, Mark 4, for 30–40 minutes until firm to touch.

Icing: Place all ingredients in mixing bowl and beat together with wooden spoon until smooth. Split cake in half and sandwich two halves together with half orange icing. Spread remaining icing over top of cake. Pipe rosettes round edge if desired.

This mixture also makes a good sponge pudding.

Lightning fruit cake

450 g (1 lb) self-raising flour
225 g (8 oz) soft brown sugar
900 g (2 lb) mixed dried fruit
12 tablespoons cooking oil
2 beaten egg whites
280 ml (½ pt) boiling skimmed milk

6275 calories
Line a 22 cm (9 in) round cake tin with greaseproof paper. Sift flour and mix in sugar and dried fruit. Stir in oil and egg whites. Stir in boiling milk and mix well. Turn into the prepared tin and bake on low shelf in oven, 350°F, 180°C, Mark 4, for 1¾–2 hours. This cake should be kept for one week before cutting.

Wartime fruit cake

1 breakfast cup syrup
1 breakfast cup sultanas
1 breakfast cup currants
1 breakfast cup skimmed milk
1 teaspoon mixed spice
pinch salt
115 g (4 oz) polyunsaturated margarine
3 breakfast cups sifted plain flour
½ teaspoon baking powder
1 teaspoon baking soda
1 tablespoon warm water

3841 calories
Boil together in a saucepan for 3 minutes the syrup, sultanas, currants, skimmed milk, mixed spice, salt and margarine. Place flour in bowl. Add baking powder. When ingredients in saucepan are cold add baking soda dissolved in warm water. Then add these ingredients to flour in basin. Mix thoroughly, place in lined and greased tin and bake in moderate oven for 1½–2 hours at 350°F, 180°C, Mark 4. Size of tin to use: 280 × 220 × 38 mm (11 × 9 × 1½ in).

Belgian fruit cake

1 cup currants and sultanas, mixed
115 g (4 oz) polyunsaturated margarine
1 cup sugar
1 cup cold tea
2 cups plain flour
pinch salt
3 level teaspoons baking powder
1 level teaspoon bicarbonate of soda
1 level teaspoon mixed spice

3255 calories
Put fruit, margarine, sugar and cold tea in saucepan, set over low heat, bring to boil and boil gently for 10 minutes, then draw pan aside to cool. Sieve together flour, salt, baking powder, soda and spice. Make well in middle of flour, add boiled fruit mixture and mix well together to make soft dough. Put into greased, lined cake tin. Bake 1½ hours at 350°F, 180°C, Mark 4. Size of tin to use: 280 × 220 × 38 mm (11 × 9 × 1½ in).

Gingerbread

280 g (10 oz) plain flour
1 teaspoon bicarbonate of soda
1½ teaspoons ginger
½ teaspoon salt
½ cup boiling water
115 g (4 oz) polyunsaturated margarine
335 g (12 oz) treacle or syrup
dried fruit may be added if liked

3225 calories
Sieve dry ingredients; melt margarine in boiling water, add syrup. Add dry ingredients and mix well. Grease 20 cm (8 in) tin, bake in moderate oven, 375°F, 190°C, Mark 5, for 40–50 minutes.

Sticky gingerbread

12 tablespoons cooking oil
450 g (1 lb) black treacle
675 g (1½ lb) plain flour
225 g (8 oz) caster sugar
½ teaspoon salt
1 teaspoon ground ginger
140 ml (¼ pt) skimmed milk
1 teaspoon bicarbonate of soda

6479 calories
Brush tin approximately 240 × 190 × 62 mm (9½ × 7½ × 2½ in) with oil and line base with grease-proof paper. Warm oil and treacle. Sift flour, salt, sugar and ground ginger together. Warm milk and stir bicarbonate of soda into it. Stir warm oil and treacle into dry ingredients and then add milk and bicarbonate of soda. Beat thoroughly. Turn into prepared tin and bake for approximately 2 hours at 325°F, 160°C, Mark 3.

Ginger-coffee crunch cake

115 g (4 oz) polyunsaturated margarine
2 tablespoons syrup
1 dessertspoon sugar
1 teaspoon ground ginger
225 g (8 oz) semi-sweet biscuits

Coffee icing:
   85 g (3 oz) polyunsaturated margarine
   225 g (8 oz) sieved icing sugar
   2 dessertspoons strong black coffee
   or 1 dessertspoon coffee essence

2673 calories
Place margarine, syrup, sugar and ginger in pan and melt gently. Crush biscuits and mix into pan. Spread mixture in prepared tin, 220 × 220 × 38 mm (9× 9× 1½ in). Allow to set and top with coffee icing. To make coffee icing: place all ingredients in a bowl, beat until smooth and then spread over cake.

Quick white cake

225 g (8 oz) sifted plain flour
1 teaspoon salt
225 g (8 oz) sugar
4 tablespoons cooking oil
8 tablespoons skimmed milk
3 teaspoons baking powder
4 egg whites
1 teaspoon vanilla

4697 calories
Prepare two 20 cm (8 in) cake tins by greasing lightly with oil or polyunsaturated margarine and dusting with flour. Sift together in mixing bowl the flour, salt and sugar. Add oil and 170 g (6 oz) of milk. Stir until flour is dampened and beat for one minute. Stir in baking powder and add remaining milk, egg whites and vanilla. Beat 2 minutes. Pour into tins and bake 25–40 minutes, 350°F, 180°C, Mark 4. These cakes may be filled with jam and iced on top.

Angel cake

85 g (3 oz) plain flour
pinch of salt
½ teaspoon cream of tartar
1 teaspoon baking powder
85 g (3 oz) cornflour
225 g (8 oz) caster sugar
skimmed milk to mix (about ½ cup)
flavouring: vanilla, orange, lemon, etc.
3 egg whites

1588 calories
Sift dry ingredients, stir in sugar. Mix with milk and add flavouring. Beat egg whites until stiff and fold in. Pour into deep, ungreased tin. Bake for about 50 minutes at 370°F, 190°C, Mark 4.

Spiced apple cake

280 g (10 oz) plain flour
3 teaspoons baking powder
30 g (1 oz) granulated sugar
¾ teaspoon salt
170 g (6 oz) polyunsaturated margarine
¾ cup skimmed milk

Topping:
  2–3 apples
  ½ teaspoon cinnamon
  30 g (1 oz) brown sugar
  40 g (1½ oz) polyunsaturated margarine

3090 calories
Sieve flour, white sugar, baking powder and salt. Rub in margarine roughly. Add milk to make soft dough. Put into ungreased 22 cm (9 in) tin. Peel, core and slice apples, arrange on top of dough. Sprinkle with brown sugar and cinnamon and dot with margarine. Bake in hot oven 30–40 minutes at 440°F, 230°C, Mark 8.

Tyrol cake

100 g (3½ oz) polyunsaturated margarine
225 g (8 oz) plain flour
1 level teaspoon ground cinnamon
55 g (2 oz) caster sugar
55 g (2 oz) currants
55 g (2 oz) sultanas
1 level teaspoon bicarbonate of soda
140 ml (¼ pt) skimmed milk
2 tablespoons clear honey

2456 calories
Grease and flour 15 cm (6 in) cake tin. Rub fat into flour and cinnamon until mixture resembles fine breadcrumbs. Stir in sugar and fruit and make well in centre. Dissolve bicarbonate of soda in some of milk, add to honey and pour into well. Gradually work in dry ingredients, adding more milk if necessary to give dropping consistency. Put into the tin and level the top. Bake in centre of warm oven, 325°F, 160°C, Mark 3, for 1¾–2 hours until well risen and firm.

Doughnut rings

170 g (6 oz) plain flour
1 level teaspoon baking powder
pinch salt
pinch nutmeg
55 g (2 oz) caster sugar
1 tablespoon cooking oil
2 egg whites
2 tablespoons skimmed milk

1063 calories
Sift all dry ingredients together into mixing bowl. Mix together oil, egg whites and milk and add to dry ingredients. Knead lightly on floured board. Roll out to 6 mm (¼ in) thickness and cut into rounds with plain 62 mm (2½ in) cutter, then remove round from centre of each with smaller cutter to form ring. Heat oil to 360°F, 185°C, and fry, turning frequently, until golden brown on both sides. Drain and sprinkle thickly with sugar.

Cherry buns

170 g (6 oz) self-raising flour
85 g (3 oz) glacé cherries
2 egg whites
85 g (3 oz) polyunsaturated margarine
115 g (4 oz) caster sugar
4 tablespoons skimmed milk
grated rind of ½ lemon

2145 calories
Sift flour, cut cherries in quarters, beat egg whites to stiff froth. Beat margarine and sugar to very soft cream; then gradually stir in milk. Add beaten egg whites. Now stir in flour and lemon rind. When quite smooth add cherries, first dusting them in a little flour to prevent them sinking in buns. Fill patty tins three-quarters full with mixture and bake at once in hot oven, 450°F, 230°C, Mark 8, for about 20 minutes. *Makes 24.*

Plain scones

225 g (8 oz) plain flour
½ teaspoon salt
2 teaspoons baking powder
1½ tablespoons cooking oil
skimmed milk to mix

1292 calories
Mix all ingredients together. Use skimmed milk to get a soft, but not wet, consistency. Roll out 12 mm (½ in) thick on floured board. Cut in rounds and bake in a hot oven, 440°F, 230°C, Mark 8, for 15 minutes.

Sultana scones

225 g (8 oz) self-raising flour
{ 1 level teaspoon cream of tartar
{ ½ level teaspoon bicarbonate of soda
or 1½ teaspoons baking powder
55 g (2 oz) sultanas
30 g (1 oz) sugar
skimmed milk to mix
1½ tablespoons cooking oil

1590 calories
Mix all ingredients together. Use skimmed milk to get a soft, but not wet, consistency. Roll out 12 mm (½ in) thick on floured board. Cut in rounds and bake in a hot oven, 440°F, 230°C, Mark 8, for 15 minutes.

Biscuits

115 g (4 oz) sugar
3 tablespoons cooking oil
170 g (6 oz) plain flour
pinch of salt
dried fruit and nuts (optional)
flavouring: vanilla, almond, orange rind, etc.

2038 calories
Mix all ingredients. Roll out and shape. Bake 15–20 minutes, 370°F, 190°C, Mark 4.

Plain biscuits

225g (8 oz) sifted Self-raising flour
½ teaspoon salt
2 tablespoons cooking oil
6 tablespoons skimmed milk

2185 calories
Sift flour, baking powder and salt together into mixing bowl. Pour oil and milk into measuring cup, but do not stir. Add all at once to flour mixture. Stir quickly with fork until dough clings together. Knead dough lightly about 10 times. Roll dough out to 3 mm ($\frac{1}{8}$ in) thick. Cut 14 biscuits with unfloured medium size cutter. Prick with fork. Place biscuits on ungreased baking sheet and bake for 12 minutes at 450°F, 230°C, Mark 8.

Cream crackers

115 g (4 oz) plain flour
1 tablespoon cooking oil
1½ tablespoons (approx.) water

984 calories
Mix all ingredients. Roll out thinly and prick. Bake for 15 minutes at 415°F, 210°C, Mark 6.

Nut crisps

115 g (4 oz) polyunsaturated margarine
85 g (3 oz) sugar
2 tablespoons golden syrup
195 g (7 oz) plain flour
55 g (2 oz) walnuts
½ teaspoon baking powder
1 teaspoon ground ginger
vanilla essence

2712 calories
Cream margarine and sugar. Add syrup, then mix in dry ingredients, flavouring and chopped walnuts. Shape into small rounds and flatten. Bake on a greased tray in a moderate oven, 350°F, 180°C, Mark 4, for 10–15 minutes.

Treacle cake

225 g (8 oz) wholemeal flour
225 g (8 oz) strong flour
2 teaspoons salt
30 g (1 oz) polyunsaturated margarine
3 tablespoons black treacle
115 g (4 oz) raisins
Yeast liquid:
   25 g (1 oz) fresh yeast
   170 ml (6 fl. oz) warm water
or
   1 teaspoon sugar
   170 ml (6 fl. oz) warm water
   3 teaspoons dried yeast

1943 calories
Blend fresh yeast in warm water *or* dissolve sugar in warm water and sprinkle on dried yeast. Leave until frothy – about 10 minutes. Place flours and salt in a bowl and rub in margarine. Blend black treacle with yeast liquid. Add to flour. Mix to firm dough. Turn on to lightly floured surface and knead for 5 minutes. Place dough in an oiled polythene bag and leave to prove for 1–1½ hours until double in size. Turn dough on to a floured surface and work in raisins until evenly distributed. Shape dough to fit a 900 g (2 lb) loaf tin. Place in oiled tin, cover with polythene and leave in a warm place until almost double in size, about 50 minutes. Bake at 450°F, 230°C, Mark 8, for 45 minutes or until loaf sounds hollow when tapped.

Rum crunchies

85 g (3 oz) polyunsaturated margarine
85 g (3 oz) caster sugar
1 egg white, large
¾ teaspoon rum essence
or 1 tablespoon Jamaica rum
85 g (3 oz) plain flour, sieved
glacé cherries to decorate, caster sugar to
   sprinkle

1439 calories
Cream margarine and sugar together until light and fluffy. Add egg white and whisk the mixture until thick and creamy (3–4 minutes). Add rum essence, or rum, then stir in flour. Place teaspoonsful of mixture well apart on lightly greased baking sheet. Press half a glacé cherry into each. Bake on middle shelf of oven, 350°F, 180°C, Mark 4, for 10–15 minutes. Cool on wire tray, then dredge with caster sugar.   *Makes 18–20.*

Nutty meringues

1 egg white
115 g (4 oz) sugar
¼ teaspoon salt
½ teaspoon vanilla
½ cup chopped walnuts
115 g (4 oz) cornflakes

1421 calories
Beat egg white in large bowl. Beat in sugar gradually. Beat in salt and vanilla. Fold in walnuts and cornflakes. Take up heaped teaspoonsful of mixture and push with another teaspoon on to well-oiled baking sheet. Bake at 300°F, 150°C, Mark 2, for about 20 minutes or until surface is dry but not brown. Remove from sheet with a knife while still warm. *Makes 24.*

Oat crisps

250 g (9 oz) rolled oats
280 g (10 oz) plain flour
½ teaspoon baking powder
½ teaspoon salt
170 g (6 oz) polyunsaturated margarine
170 g (6 oz) brown sugar
½ cup water

Filling:
   170 g (6 oz) raisins
   55 g (2 oz) sugar
   30 g (1 oz) polyunsaturated margarine

5120 calories
Sieve flour, salt and baking powder, and add oats. Cream margarine and sugar. Add dry ingredients alternately with water. Chill. Roll out to 2 mm (½ in) thickness and cut into rounds. Bake on greased tin in moderate oven, 350°F, 180°C, Mark 4, for 10 minutes. Allow to cool. Meanwhile make filling. Heat filling ingredients gently in pan. Allow to cool, then use as sandwich filling between the biscuits.

Fruity almond squares

2 egg whites
115 g (4 oz) icing sugar
85 g (3 oz) self-raising flour
½ teaspoon salt
55 g (2 oz) ground almonds
few drops almond essence
3 tablespoons cooking oil
115 g (4 oz) stoned dates, chopped
115 g (4 oz) mixed peel

2138 calories
Brush shallow tin approximately 20 cm (8 in) square or 25 × 15 cm (10 × 6 in) oblong with oil. Whisk the egg whites slightly then whisk in the sugar 55 g (2 oz) at a time until mixture thickens. Sift flour and salt together. Gradually fold into egg-white mixture with ground almonds, almond essence and oil. Fold in dates and mixed peel. Turn into a prepared tin and bake at 325°F, 160°C, Mark 3, for 35 minutes. Cut into squares while still warm. Allow to cool before removing from the tin. *Makes 16.*

Butterscotch fingers

195 g (7 oz) plain flour
¼ teaspoon salt
170 g (6 oz) soft brown sugar
6 tablespoons cooking oil
1 egg white
1 teaspoon vanilla essence

Topping:
    170 g (6 oz) butterscotch sweets
    1½ tablespoons cooking oil
    1 tablespoon water
    ¼ teaspoon salt

3174 calories

To make topping, place butterscotch sweets in oil, water and salt in a basin over boiling water and melt gradually; this will take approximately 45 minutes. Brush shallow tin, approximately 28 × 18 × 2·5 cm (12 × 7 × 1 in), with oil. Sift flour and salt together and mix in sugar. Stir in oil, egg white and vanilla essence; mix well together. Turn into prepared tin and bake at 350°F, 180°C, Mark 4, for 20 minutes. Allow to cool slightly, then spread topping over biscuit. Allow the topping to set, then cut into fingers.   *Makes 20.*

Shortbread

{ 115 g (4 oz) plain flour
{ 55 g (2 oz) rice flour
or 170 g (6 oz) plain flour
55 g (2 oz) caster sugar
115 g (4 oz) polyunsaturated margarine

1795 calories

Rub fat into flour and sugar. Knead well. Roll out 2 mm (⅛ in) thick, prick well. Cut out and bake in cool oven, 300°F, 150°C, Mark 3, for 20 minutes.

Shortcake

200 g (7 oz) plain flour
30 g (1 oz) cornflour
55 g (2 oz) caster sugar
30 g (1 oz) icing sugar
4 tablespoons cooking oil

2436 calories

Sieve flour and cornflour. Add sugar, stir in oil. Press into 18 cm (7 in) greased tin and bake for 1 hour at 350°F, 180°C, Mark 4.

Ginger crunch

115 g (4 oz) polyunsaturated margarine
115 g (4 oz) sugar
1 large teacup plain flour
½ teaspoon baking powder
½ teaspoon ground ginger

Icing:
  4 tablespoons icing sugar
  3 teaspoons golden syrup
  2 tablespoons polyunsaturated margarine
  1 teaspoon ground ginger

2876 calories
Cream margarine and sugar and add sieved dry ingredients. Press mixture into thin layer in a shallow greased tin and bake for 20–30 minutes in a moderate oven, 350°F, 180°C, Mark 4.

Icing: heat all ingredients together in pan until they are melted and beat thoroughly. Pour icing over crunch while both are still warm. Cut into squares before completely cold.

Brandy snaps

2 level tablespoons golden syrup
55 g (2 oz) polyunsaturated margarine
40 g (1½ oz) caster sugar
40 g (1½ oz) plain flour, sifted
½ level teaspoon ground ginger

1023 calories
Grease two large baking sheets. Put syrup, margarine and sugar into heavy-based pan. Heat gently until all ingredients have dissolved. Remove from heat, beat in flour and ginger until smooth. Drop teaspoons of mixture 5 cm (2 in) apart, on prepared baking sheets. Bake in two batches, in centre of pre-heated oven, 400°F, 200°C, Mark 6, for 5–6 minutes each, or until golden brown. Meanwhile grease handle of wooden spoon. Leave snaps to cool very slightly on baking sheet. Remove carefully with palette knife and wrap each one round handle of wooden spoon. Remove, and put on wire rack to finish cooling. Store in airtight tin. *Makes 10.*

Flapjacks

170 g (6 oz) polyunsaturated margarine
55 g (2 oz) soft brown sugar
3 tablespoons golden syrup
335 g (12 oz) rolled oats
¼ level teaspoon salt

3270 calories
Grease an 18 × 28 cm (7 × 11 in) Swiss roll tin with oil. Put margarine and sugar in mixing bowl. Beat well until soft and fluffy. Heat syrup gently in small pan. Beat into creamed mixture. Beat in oats and salt. Spread mixture in prepared tin and bake in the centre of a pre-heated oven, 400°F, 200°C, Mark 6, for 30 minutes or until golden brown. While mixture is still hot, cut into fingers but leave in tin to complete cooling; remove very carefully. *Makes 14.*

Eating Guide

Use this guide as a handy reference when selecting food. People already under the care of their doctor and dietitian should check first. The guide can then be approved and used as an adjunct to their existing eating pattern.

1   For people who don't need to watch their weight.

However, it is still important not to get overweight by eating too much.

Low fat, low saturated fat, low cholesterol diet. No calorie limit.

Daily allowance: 560 ml (1 pt) skimmed milk – more if wished.
low fat natural yoghurt as wished.
30–40 ml (2–3 tablespoons) oil – safflower, sunflower, corn, soya bean.
30 g (1 oz) polyunsaturated margarine.

Weekly allowance: 1 whole egg (standard size).

Allowed
Dairy products: Skimmed milk, low fat yoghurt, egg white, plain ice cream, cottage cheese.
Fats: Polyunsaturated margarine, oils – safflower, sunflower, corn, soya bean.
Meat, poultry, fish: Small portions of lean meat, i.e. beef, lamb, pork, ham, bacon. Medium portions of chicken, rabbit, turkey, veal. Large portions of white fish, smoked haddock.
Soup: Clear soups i.e. consommé, broths, purée or cream soups made using oil or polyunsaturated margarine.
Cereals: All breakfast and pudding, pastas.
Breads, pastries, biscuits: Any prepared with suitable fat or egg white.
Puddings: Any prepared with skimmed milk or suitable fats. Meringues (no cream), jellies, sorbets.
Vegetables and fruit: All (fresh, frozen, tinned, dried). Potatoes to be cooked in suitable margarine or oil.
Miscellaneous: Tea, coffee, fruit squashes, minerals, salt, pepper, herbs, spices. In moderation sugar, jam, marmalade, honey, boiled sweets, walnuts, almonds.

Forbidden
Dairy products: Whole milk, including sterilized, Jersey, UHT, evaporated, full cream dried. Cream, mock cream, coffee creamers, sour cream, butter, other cheeses, whole egg, egg yolk, Cornish, dairy or fancy ice creams.
Fats: Other margarines, lard, dripping, suet, cooking fats, meat fats, coconut and palm oil.
Meat, poultry, fish: All fatty meats, mince, sausages, fatty cold meats, i.e. salami, luncheon meat, goose, duck, game and high cholesterol meats and fish.
Soup: Greasy soups, soups except those made with polyunsaturated oil and margarine. *Watch* tinned and packet varieties.
Cereals: Egg noodles.
Breads, pastries, biscuits: Those prepared with forbidden fats or egg yolks. Doughnuts, cream cakes, bought cakes and biscuits, including cake mixes.
Puddings: Those prepared with forbidden fats or egg yolks. Pancakes, suet pudding, bought pastries.
Vegetables: Potato crisps, potatoes cooked in forbidden fats. *Watch* bought chips or when eating out.
Miscellaneous: Mayonnaise, salad cream, malted milk drinks, chocolate, cashew nuts, coconut.

2   For slimmers

Low calorie, low fat, low saturated fat, low cholesterol diet.
1500 calorie limit.

Daily Allowance: 560 ml (1 pt) skimmed milk or 420 ml (¾ pt) skimmed milk plus 140 g (5 oz) low fat natural yoghurt.
15 ml (1 tablespoon) oil – safflower, sunflower, corn, soya bean.
15 g (½ oz) polyunsaturated margarine.
7 portions from the Bread Exchange List, *see* page 125.

Weekly allowance: 1 whole egg (standard size).

Allowed
Dairy products: Skimmed milk and low fat natural yoghurt allowance.
Fats: Polyunsaturated margarine, oil allowance.

Meat, poultry, fish: Small portions of lean meat. Medium portions of chicken, turkey, rabbit, veal. Large portions of white fish and smoked haddock.

Soups: Clear soups, broths and unthickened purée soups.

Bread, cereals, biscuits: 7 portions from the Bread Exchange List, *see* page 125.

Vegetables: Potatoes boiled, mashed or jacket, and dried vegetables from allowance. Salads, green vegetables (fresh, frozen, tinned), root vegetables, peas (small portion).

Fruits: Fresh or fresh stewed, fresh fruit salad, baked apple or pears. Tinned fruit in water. Four portions per day.

Miscellaneous: Saccharine and a little crystal fructose or lactose sweetener. Tea, coffee, low calorie squashes and minerals, salt, pepper, herbs, spices.

Forbidden

Dairy products: Whole milk, including sterilized, Jersey, UHT, evaporated, condensed, full cream dried. Cream, mock cream, coffee creamers, sour cream, butter, other cheeses, whole egg, egg yolk, ice cream.

Fats: Other margarines, lard, dripping, suet, cooking fat, meat fat, coconut and palm oil.

Meat, poultry, fish: All fatty meats, mince, sausages, luncheon meats, salami, goose, duck, game and high cholesterol meats and fish.

Soup: Greasy soups and those containing thickening and whole milk solids.

Cereals, pastries, biscuits: All, including cakes, pastries, sweet biscuits, Yorkshire pudding. Bread apart from ration.

Vegetables: Starchy vegetables and potatoes apart from ration.

Fruits: Sweetened, tinned (in sugar or sorbitol), dried.

Miscellaneous: Sugar, glucose, chocolate, cocoa, malted drinks, sweets, nuts, jam, marmalade, honey, sauces, salad cream, mayonnaise.

WORKING OUT PORTIONS

These portion lists can be used by people on special diets. It is important to check with your own doctor and dietitian first to ensure this is in line with their advice.

Bread Exchange List – Useful for slimmers

The food portions listed here provide equivalent energy to one slice of bread, i.e. 70 calories (294 kilojoules).

30 g (1 oz) bread: white, brown, French and low-starch (= 1 large thin round)

85 g (3 oz) potato: plain boiled or mashed

3 pieces of crispbread

20 g (¾ oz) plain breakfast cereal, i.e individual pack or 1 teacup Corn Flakes/Rice Crispies or 1½ Weetabix *or* 1 Shredded Wheat

20 g (¾ oz) raw rice *or* 55 g (2 oz) boiled rice

20 g (¾ oz) raw spaghetti or other pasta *or* 75 g (2½ oz) cooked pasta

20 g (¾ oz) dry breadcrumbs

85 g (3 oz) sweetcorn (off the cob)

85 g (3 oz) baked beans

30 g (1 oz) raw haricot/black eye/kidney beans *or* butter beans *or* lentils

Carbohydrate Portions – For people on carbohydrate restricted diets (*see* Introduction page 10).

Each one of you will have your own carbohydrate portion list to use to add variety to your meals. This is a small list of useful items which will help you to use the recipes in this book.

Food fried in breadcrumbs or batter (if batter is eaten)	= 10 g C
4 dessertspoons white sauce or thick gravy	= 10 g C
30 g (1 oz) thickening, i.e. flour, cornflour, breadcrumbs	= 20 g C
20 g (¾ oz) skimmed milk powder, i.e. 3 rounded (5 ml) teaspoons	= 10 g C
195 ml (7 oz) liquid skimmed milk	= 10 g C

SUGGESTIONS FOR PLANNING MEALS

These meal plans give a good idea of how to vary meals when using a good hearted diet. The plan allows for one light meal and one main meal, plus breakfast.

Breakfasts

Cereal, fresh or tinned grapefruit, apples, prunes or rhubarb. Fruit juice. Tea or coffee with skimmed milk. Bread, toast or crispbread, polyunsaturated margarine and marmalade or jam.

Winter meals

Sunday: Light meal – *baked stuffed potatoes; apricots in syrup.

Main meal – roast beef and Yorkshire pudding, vegetables in season; *apple shortcake.

Monday: Light meal – cottage pie; fresh fruit.

Main meal – *spiced gammon steaks, broccoli and savoury rice; *apple mousse.

Tuesday: Light meal – *Cornish pasties, water biscuits; celery and cottage cheese.

Main meal – *Spanish cod, carrots, creamed potatoes; *pancakes and orange sauce.

Wednesday: Light meal – *cottage cheese and ham rarebit; fresh fruit.

Main meal – *Romany chicken, runner beans, boiled potatoes; *lemon sherbert.

Thursday: Light meal – savoury minced beef pie; carton of low fat yoghurt with soft brown sugar.

Main meal – *lemon ginger chops, brussels sprouts, sauté potatoes; *surprise meringue.

Friday: Light meal – *Scotch broth and wholemeal bread; fresh fruit.

Main meal – fried haddock, tomato sauce, peas and chips; *pineapple fluff.

Saturday: Light meal – *cauliflower casserole, wholemeal bread; cottage cheese.

Main meal – beef stew with dumplings, cabbage, creamed potatoes: *fruit whip.

*Find starred recipes in this book.

Summer meals

Sunday: Light meal – *ham ring mould, green salad, wholemeal bread.

Main meal – roast chicken, bread sauce, stuffing, roast potatoes, runner beans; *summer pudding and *ice cream.

Monday: Light meal – chicken risotto; cottage cheese and water biscuits.

Main meal – *paupiettes of plaice, creamed potatoes, peas; rhubarb crumble and custard.

Tuesday: Light meal – cottage cheese salad; fresh fruit.

Main meal – *goulash, braised courgettes, new potatoes; *apple or strawberry flan.

Wednesday: Light meal – fish cakes and chips; fresh fruit.

Main meal – *carbonnade of lamb, runner beans, new potatoes; *lemon sorbet.

Thursday: Light meal – *bacon flan; carton of low fat yoghurt.

Main meal – *devilled chicken, carrots, savoury rice; *fruit salad and *flummery.

Friday: Light meal – cottage cheese and pineapple salad, bread.

Main meal – *stuffed marrow and creamed potatoes; fresh strawberries and *ice cream.

Saturday   Light meal – soused herrings and salad; wholemeal bread and cottage cheese.

Main meal – *pork and cider casserole, broad beans, new potatoes; *baked bananas and lemon sauce.

Index